Politics
and the African
Development Bank

Politics
and the African
Development Bank

Karen A. Mingst

THE UNIVERSITY PRESS OF KENTUCKY

Library of Congress Cataloging-in-Publication Data

Mingst, Karen A., 1947-
    Politics and the African development bank / Karen A. Mingst.
        p.   cm.
    Includes bibliographical references.
    ISBN 0-8131-1754-2
    1. African Development Bank.   2. Africa—Politics and
government—1960-   I. Title.
HG3881.5.A37M56   1990
332.1'53'096—dc20   90-30935

Contents

Tables and Figure

Figure

Acknowledgments

The idea of a project on the African Development Bank (ADB) emerged from a paper I wrote comparing American influence in the regional development banks; I discovered in that research virtually no published information on the ADB. Two weeks after the idea had been translated into a proposal submitted to the Fulbright Program, our second child was conceived. Children inevitably develop faster and with a degree of biological determination not found in the maturation of an intellectual idea. Hence the field research of this book was postponed until after the birth of my son, Brett.

Research was conducted in both Washington, D.C., and Abidjan, Ivory Coast, as well as in Senegal, Ivory Coast, Niger, and Burkina Faso. Partial financial assistance for the United States portion of the research was received from the University of Kentucky Research Foundation; generous support for the African portion was provided by the Fulbright Sub-Saharan Africa Fellowship Program. Particular thanks to U.S. Information Agency personnel, especially Willie Holmes, who provided logistical support and encouragement. Thanks also to the African Development Bank's former secretary general, M. L. Yuma, who made individuals at the African Development Bank accessible, and to Mme. S. Diarra, who graciously gave me administrative support, intervening on my behalf "to get" the information and interviews. Our long informal conversations about life in Africa added special insight to my sojourn. The numerous persons interviewed in West Africa—including ADB personnel, contractors, private bankers—and Washington, D.C., officials agreed to be cited anonymously. Information gleaned from these individuals is integrated into the text without attribution. While in the Ivory Coast, I also benefited from the companionship of a fellow Fulbrighter, Nancy Lawler, whose historical research at the village level introduced me to "village" Africa in northern Ivory Coast and Burkina Faso. Kim Hayden of the Department of Political Science at the University of Kentucky expertly typed and revised too many drafts; I hope she still remains my friend.

Earlier versions of several chapters were presented at professional meetings of the International Studies Association and the Midwest Political Science Association; an expanded version of chapter 7 appeared in the *Review of International Studies* (1987, 13:281-93). An earlier draft of chapter 10 was presented at the University of Chicago's seminar on International Politics, Economics, and Security. In each forum, the manuscript was improved by the comments of others.

Our son is now five years old. For making it this far, I owe special gratitude to my parents, Richard and Edna Mingst, who "toddler sat" in California while I was in Africa and while my husband, Robert Stauffer, was finishing a project at the University of Maine. Although their friends thought them crazy, my mother's real motivation is revealing: "Since you were six years old, all you've talked about is Africa, but my young grandchildren are *not* going there."

Only another academic understands why one does these things. My husband understands fascination, although his own is with the natural world of lakes and water. He has endured this project and all the others since our graduate-school days. I have been with him, too, with stints in Wisconsin, California, Maine, and Yugoslavia.

I dedicate this book to Ginger and Brett—that they may experience the wonders of a multicultural world.

Glossary

ADB	African Development Bank
ADF	African Development Fund
AID (USAID)	Agency for International Development (United States)
APPER	Africa's Priority Program for Economic Recovery
CEAO	West African Economic Community
CFA	Unit of currency for African states in the Franc zone
ECA	Economic Commission for Africa (United Nations)
ECOWAS	Economic Community of West African States
EFF	Extended Fund Facility
FAO	Food and Agriculture Organization (United Nations)
FSO	Fund for Special Operations
IBRD	International Bank for Reconstruction and Development (also known as the World Bank)
ICAO	International Civil Aviation Organization
IDA	International Development Association
IDB	Inter-American Development Bank
IFAD	International Fund for Agricultural Development
IFC	International Finance Corporation
IGOs	international governmental organizations
IMF	International Monetary Fund
MDBs	multilateral development banks
NTF	Nigerian Trust Fund
OAU	Organization of African Unity
OECD	Organization for Economic Cooperation and Development
OPEC	Organization of Petroleum Exporting Countries
PANAFTEL	Pan African Telecommunications
PIR	Public Investment Review

REDSO	Regional Economic Development Services Office (United States' AID)
SAL	Structural Adjustment Lending
SIDA	Swedish International Development Authority
UA	Units of account
UN	United Nations
UNDP	United Nations Development Program
UNESCO	United Nations Educational, Scientific and Cultural Organization
UNIDO	United Nations Industrial Development Organization
UN-PAAERD	United Nations Programme of Action for African Economic Recovery and Development
USAID	*See* AID
WB	World Bank (*See also* IBRD)
WHO	World Health Organization

CHAPTER 1 ─────────────────────────────

Introduction

─────────────────────────────

The rejuvenation of international organizations (IGOs) as a field of study can be attributed to several trends in the international political system: the increasing proliferation of IGOs and the resulting complexity of national entanglements in these organizations (Jacobson, Reisinger and Mathers, 1986; Nierop, 1989); the interrelatedness of issues that the various organizations address; and the increasing fragmentation of institutional responses (Cox, 1980). The renewal of inquiry has led scholars to ask some critical questions: How have the patterns of influence between IGOs and state members changed over time (Karns and Mingst, 1990)? What is the impact of interorganizational relations in an era of multiple institutional responses (Jönsson, 1986; Mingst, 1987; Ness and Brechin, 1988)? What is the IGO's impact on specific international and domestic issues (Mingst and Schechter, 1985; Finkelstein, 1988; Frenkle and O'Donnell, 1979; Hoole, 1977)? And on state's foreign policy (Karns and Mingst, 1987)? What roles can international organizations play both in institutionalizing and in challenging hegemony (Cox, 1980)? And how do international organizations fit into the broader patterns of international regimes and governance (Kratochwil and Ruggie, 1986; Snidal, 1990)?

These questions correspond to different analytical foci in the study of international organizations. As an actor, IGOs are involved in a two-way flow of influence with state members; they interact with similar organizations; they affect the allocation of values and distribution of resources on specific issues; they influence the process and the substantive policies of a state's foreign policy. They serve as actors capable of both reinforcing and diluting hegemonic power. They fit into a broader pattern of governance by playing key roles in the creation and maintenance of regimes, and contributing to the formation, continuity, and stability of "habits of cooperation" (Rosenau, 1986). "Because of their trappings of universality," international organizations "are the major venues within which the global legitimation struggle over international regimes is carried out today" (Kratochwil and Ruggie, 1986:773). Underlying each of these analytical foci is an implicit recognition that IGOs are political institutions.

As political institutions, IGO members represent states whose governments make policy choices; many states call for IGO decisions affecting national and global interests. Within these organizations, states have differing interests—philosophical conflicts over appropriate courses of action and conflicts over narrowly defined political interests (Williams, 1987:55). Politics has always existed and will continue to persist.

Specialized international organizations based on functionalist logic were developed to minimize politics as much as possible. Indeed, the theory of functionalism posited that technical functions could be separated from political functions and that these technical functions would best be "housed" in appropriate nonpolitical forums (Mitrany, 1943). The multilateral development banks (MDBs) have since their founding embraced the functionalist logic that technical economic questions could be separable from political questions. This doctrine has been encapsulated in the doctrine of economic neutrality.

In the *Articles of Agreement of the International Bank for Reconstruction and Development* (World Bank, 1945), the relevant provisions for economic neutrality are stated,

The Bank shall make arrangements to ensure that the proceeds of any loan are used for the purposes for which the loan was granted with due attention to considerations of economy and efficiency and without regard to political or other non-economic influences or considerations. [Art. III, sec. 5b]

The Bank and its officers shall not interfere in the political affairs of any member; nor shall they be influenced in their decisions by the political character of the member or members concerned. Only economic considerations shall be relevant to their decisions, and these considerations shall be weighed impartially in order to achieve the purposes stated in Article I. [Art. IV, sec. 10]

In a similar vein, in the *Agreement Establishing the African Development Bank* (African Development Bank, 1981a), Article 38 stipulates the following:

The Bank shall not accept loans or assistance that could in any way prejudice, limit, deflect or otherwise alter its purpose or functions.

The Bank, its President, Vice-Presidents, officers and staff shall not interfere in the political affairs of any member; nor shall they be influenced in their decisions by the political character of the member concerned. Only economic considerations shall be relevant to their decisions. Such considerations shall be weighed impartially in order to achieve and carry out the functions of the Bank.

The President, Vice-Presidents, officers and staff of the Bank, in discharge of their offices, owe their duty entirely to the Bank and to no other authority. Each member of the Bank shall respect the international character of this duty and shall refrain from all attempts to influence any of them in the discharge of their duties.

Even as recently as 1982, World Bank officials confirmed publicly that they should not address political questions, and they do not. What the Bank promotes is simply sound economic and financial management, technocratically orchestrated.

The doctrine of economic neutrality has usefully served the interests of a number of different constituencies. The myth that technical expertise guides organizational policy enhances the power of IGO officials and administrators. They are the acknowledged experts whose recommendations are to be followed. Leaders of Third World member states find it expedient to hide behind the shield of the MDB's economic neutrality when announcing domestic austerity measures, justifying politically unpopular measures on the basis of neutral and nonpolitical reasons (Swedberg, 1986:377, 388-90). These countries have generally assumed that "economic advice from the multilateral institutions . . . [be] more technical and less political than advice from bilateral donors" (U.S. House of Representatives, 1985). Even the advanced industrial states, the major donors, have found the myth that the organizations could and should function as economic, nonpolitical institutions self-serving. In 1968, for example, Joseph Barr, then Treasury Under-secretary, asserted, "They [the banks] cannot be looked on as an extension of our diplomacy. They are designed purely for development and the betterment of these developing nations" (U.S. Senate, Foreign Relations Committee, 1968:5).

To perpetuate the apolitical myth, bank officials "call political factors by other names" (Spiro, 1979:147). They have developed and/or revised procedures including regularizing consensus voting for approving loans and having one executive director represent a group of countries to try to avoid the formation of power blocs. They have promoted a research and consultant system to enhance the credibility of the institutions as technical bodies (Hürni, 1980:12-13).

Early research on the development banks confirmed the apolitical nature of the institutions. Edward S. Mason and Robert E. Asher (1973) and Robert W. Oliver (1975) each wrote authoritative accounts of the World Bank Group of institutions, discussing in detail their origin and evolution. Sidney Dell (1972), John White (1972), and Po Wen Huang (1975) followed the same approach in their respective analyses of the regional banks, although in White's case, the information base for the comparative assessment was inadequate. Babutana M. Mvioki (1985), Paul Pratt (1982), and Hussan M. Selim (1983) each conducted a descriptive and legalistic analysis of their subject, perpetuating the myth that these organizations are apolitical bodies.

Drawing upon the observations of David A. Baldwin (1965) that the World Bank is a political institution since bank loans affect domestic priorities and distribution of power, a number of writers began systematically to dispel the myth of economic neutrality, both in terms of interactions within the organization and between the organization and its major donors. Bettin S. Hürni (1980) explores how borrowing governments are affected by the political side of projects, gaining votes in elections, and advancing group interests. She concludes, "The political factors point out that the standard parameters, definitions, and criteria used by the Bank might be somewhat one-sided in that they apply to economic conditions only" (1980:118). Robert Ayres (1983) assesses how the controversial changes in Bank policy toward poverty alleviation affected relations among bank managers and the extent to which the reorientation resulted in changes in borrowing countries. R. Peter DeWitt, Jr. (1977) and Cheryl Payer (1982), too, are more interested in assessing impact, but both begin from the premise that the banks are essentially exploitive tools of the Western industrializers. Not surprisingly, each finds that the banks have a political and economic effect on borrowing member states, which tends to perpetuate the power of the ruling elite. Subsequent research on other international economic organizations—global (Rothstein, 1979), regional (Daltrop, 1986), or issue-specific (Fisher, 1972; Mikdashi, 1972)—has continued to explode the myth of economic neutrality and with it the fundamental notion of functionalism.

International economic organizations, though their areas of competence be limited in content and technically specialized, are indeed political institutions. In the literature on the multilateral development banks, most attention is given to how the economic hegemons, the largest donors, use the organization to further their individual political and economic interests. But the findings are inconclusive and incomplete. To Jonathan E. Sanford (1982), the United States strongly influences but does not politically control the various banks. His evidence focuses on how divisions within American domestic structures, particularly conflicts between the executive and legislative branches, circumscribe America's ability to exert political control. To Dennis T. Yasutomo (1983), the Asian Development Bank is a direct tool of Japanese national interest. In contrast, Stephen D. Krasner (1981) compares different types of contributions by the larger donors and finds these donors do not enjoy voting influence commensurate with the amount of their contributions. But these studies offer confirmatory evidence that economic hegemons in the multilateral development banks act to further their political interests.

Other issues have not been as thoroughly addressed in the literature on multilateral development banks as international economic organizations. How do hegemons use their influence? Are they effective? What other political factors intervene to erode further the myth of economic neutrality? With the increase in numbers of personnel employed in these organizations due to the enlargement of state members, has political controversy been exacerbated? What effect has the increase in number of issues falling under the multilateral development bank's jurisdiction had on political relationships? Has the proliferation of other IGOs resulted in a more politically controversial environment? Exploration of these questions permits us to examine systematically how one multilateral development bank, the African Development Bank, came to be an "ordinary" IGO, infused with political controversy in the organizational and interorganizational arenas.

Attention to arenas and levels of political conflict within an organization permits us to cross the analytical foci dominant in the field of international organization. In dispelling the doctrine of economic neutrality so pervasive in the formal institutional structure of the multilateral development banks, we rediscover the utility of examining structures and analyzing organizational behavior. We discover what roles the organizations could play in creatively solving substantive problems. We explore the extent to which these organizations only reflect hegemonic interests or could actually undermine hegemonic power.

This book examines politics in one such international economic organization, the African Development Bank group. This bank, comparable to other multilateral development banks, lends money based on "sound banking practices" for projects that are "technically, financially and economically viable" (Gardiner and Pickett, 1984:70). In addition, the projects funded must be of a developmental nature, contributing in the long term to economic growth. The research is based on the proposition that the African Development Bank, like the much-studied World Bank (International Bank for Reconstruction and Development, WB or IBRD) and Inter-American Development

Bank (IDB), is basically a political institution. In contrast to the plethora of material written about the International Bank for Reconstruction and Development (Ayres, 1983; Hürni, 1980; Oliver, 1975; Payer, 1982) and the Inter-American Development Bank (Dell, 1972; DeWitt, 1977), both the Asian Development Bank and the African Development Bank have been woefully understudied.

The earliest descriptive account of the African Development Bank was written by Yewom Charles Amégavie in 1977. Although this thesis offers a thorough account of the early debate over the creation of the ADB, including such issues as membership and location, its assessment of programs effectively terminates in 1973. In the words of Amégavie, the Bank had just ended the "phase of hesitation and caution" and was embarking on an extension of activities.

Kwame Donkoh Fordwor (1981), a former president of the Bank, offers an illuminating and thought-provoking analysis of the ADB. Unfortunately, because Fordwor's descriptions of the personal animosities and the quarrels among the state representatives to the ADB are designed to vindicate himself in his dispute with the executive directors, an objective assessment of the dynamic relationship between the organization and state members is absent. While the preparatory debates over the admission of the extraregional members are discussed, and how Fordwor himself was so instrumental to the process, the 1981 publication date does not permit us to see how the organization fared with the admission of the extraregionals.

More recently, Gardiner and Pickett (1984) wrote an "official" history of the Bank, a useful overview of structure and activities, focusing on the Bank as an *economic* institution. Politics both within the institution and between the management and member states is scarcely mentioned; controversy is evidently not part of the "official history." Babutana M. Mvioki (1985) examines the legal statutes of the African Development Fund (ADF), focusing on how the law applicable to loan accords of the Fund are applied. Unfortunately, little is proffered about the critical question of the effects of extraregional membership in the Bank or the Fund.

Other studies offer comparisons among the multilateral development institutions, including the African Development Bank. For example, Sanford (1982) and Lars Schoultz (1982) examine the MDBs including the ADB in the context of American foreign policy; similarly, Krasner (1981) compares the relationship between voting power and contributions of the various banks. Pratt (1982) and Selim (1983) each devote one descriptive chapter to the African Development Bank as part of their cataloging of international financial institutions. With the least known about the ADB, the least is written. What is written tends to be strictly legalistic, serving to perpetuate the myth that international economic organizations are apolitical bodies.

This work analyzes changing political relationships in the African Development Bank following the adhesion of the extraregional member states. The Bank maintains the objectives outlined in the founding agreement:

1. To finance investment projects and programs which promote the economic and social development of members, giving special priority to those which concern several members, render their economies increasingly complementary, and bring about an orderly expansion in their foreign trade.
2. To undertake the preparation and selection of activities contributing to such development.
3. To mobilize resources in Africa and outside Africa for this purpose.
4. To provide technical assistance for the preparation, financing, and execution of development projects and programs.
5. To promote, generally, investment in Africa of public and private capital.
6. To cooperate with national, subregional, and regional development institutions in Africa in the fulfillment of these objectives. [African Development Bank 1981a]

Changes have occurred, however, in the economic and political resources of the Bank, as well as in the types of salient political issues.

Political relationships are analyzed in three different arenas. Intraorganizational politics occurs as the result of interactions within the organization among the president, secretariat, and member representatives. Interorganizational politics occurs among borrowing member states competing for scarce economic resources, among donor states seeking procurement contracts, and among competing international organizations. And hegemonic politics results from economic and political power exercised by hegemonic actors in the other two arenas. Such powers are not necessarily malevolent or benevolent, but being economically strong and politically willful, these states can exercise considerable influence.

ADB monetary resources are separated into ordinary capital resources and special resources. The former includes subscribed capital, bank borrowings against callable capital, and income from guarantees and loans. The latter includes the special funds and income from these operations. The Bank's capitalization in 1964 was $300 million, of which one-half was to be paid in convertible currency. Initially, numerous countries had difficulty in meeting this paid-in obligation. The portion that was callable did little to generate additional funds because, according to Krasner (1981:323), the international financial markets were unwilling to accept it as collateral for bond issues. In these beginning years, the lending program was financed exclusively by its paid-in capital stock.

Since 1973 the Bank has augmented its capital base by external borrowings. The Austrian, Canadian, and Swedish governments, as well as the Organization of Petroleum Exporting Countries (OPEC), made concessional loans to the Bank. From 1975 to 1982 the Bank began a more extensive period of external borrowing through both bond and Euro-currency markets, numbering thirty separate borrowing transactions. As reported in Gardiner and Pickett, "Of the total amounts thus raised, only 5 percent came from bilateral loans and the floatation of bonds subscribed by Central Banks. The remainder accrued from transactions in the private markets, with Euro-credit and related borrowings accounting for 70 percent of the funds raised, and the Tokyo and German capital markets each providing 11 percent" (1984:51).

In 1982 the economic resources of the Bank were significantly augmented. Acting on data that the Bank would be un-

Table 1. Selected Growth Indicators, African Development
Bank Group, 1974-86 ($1,000)

End of	Number of staff	ADB called paid-up capital[1]	ADF subscriptions	NTF resources	Annual	
					Loan approvals	Dis-bursements
1974	273	$ 171,106	$ 89,621	$ —	$ 135,511	$ 23,996
1976	336	228,621	339,890	40,840	179,409	61,961
1978	505	364,020	489,490	90,841	423,483	141,888
1980	689	382,320	1,332,153	111,907	570,836	220,083
1981	724	396,679	1,251,125	181,163	635,532	200,131
1982	774	451,210	1,789,758	202,167	765,819	280,249
1983	829	645,955	2,140,630	217,859	898,718	352,957
1984	861	792,368	2,053,844	247,987	879,264	288,599
1985	902	1,117,583	3,449,190	280,314	1,154,062	531,047
1986	994	1,459,713	4,290,878	305,357	1,640,326	672,319

[1]Called paid-up capital is equal to the subscribed capital less callable capital
and less uncalled paid-up portion.

Source: African Develpment Bank Planning and Research Department. *Compendium of Statistics*, (1984, 1987).

able to increase its economic base sufficiently to meet the
development needs of its members without participation from
non-African states, the African membership voted to invite
extraregional membership. This expansion of membership (the
conditions of which will be discussed in detail in chapter 4)
meant an increase in the capital of the Bank. Between 1981 and
1982, the authorized capital of the Bank increased by more than
120%. This included the initial subscriptions by extraregionals
and an increase of 76.6% in subscription capital by regional
members (Gardiner and Pickett, 1984:57).

Table 1 shows selected growth indicators of economic resources for the ADB. Substantial increases of economic resources occurred over a relatively short period of time. In 1986,
lending expanded by 42% and in 1987 it is estimated that the
capital base of the Bank tripled to $22 billion (Whitaker,
1988:203). For the 1987-91 period, the Bank has committed itself
to investing $12.3 billion in Africa, more than in the previous
years combined (Thurow, 1989:11).

These economic resources are used for loans to member states. Applying sound banking principles, the Bank disburses funds at market rate with maturities ranging between twelve and twenty years. The financing is meant to cover the foreign exchange expenditures incurred on a project, generally less than one-half of the project's cost.

In addition to the African Development Bank, the African Development Bank group consists of two facilities for concessionary funds. The most important is the African Development Fund, established in 1972, with the Bank and twenty extraregional states as members. The resources of the Fund consist of contributions from the extraregional members and the Bank, funds that are periodically replenished. Japan and the United States together account for more than one-quarter of all subscriptions; and along with Canada, the Federal Republic of Germany, and Italy contribute one-half of the funding. Loans from the Fund are made with repayment periods of fifty years and a service charge of .75% per annum. Such loans are designed to finance infrastructure in the poorer member countries. Table 2 shows the growth of ADF economic resources. During the 1980s, the Fund has become increasingly important to many African countries that cannot afford the Bank's market interest charges. For example in 1987, the Fund approved loans for thirty-one sub-Saharan countries totaling $766 million; by contrast, only ten countries borrowed from the Bank ($694 million).

It was anticipated that economic resources to the Bank group would also be augmented by Special Funds designed to serve specific functions. The Nigerian Trust Fund (NTF) became operational in 1976, with an initial subscription of Naira 50 million. When available, these funds are loaned to states on terms intermediate between Bank and Fund conditions: an interest rate of four percent; repayment period of twenty-five years, including a five-year grace period; and a commitment fee of .75% per annum. Nigerian replenishment of the fund, however, has been sporadic and well below expectations.

Two other special funds are part of the economic resources of the Bank group, the Arab Oil Fund and the Special Relief Fund, designed specifically for aid to drought-stricken African coun-

Table 2. Selected Growth Indicators, African Development Fund (UA '000)

End of	Participants	Total (1+2+3+4)	Initial subscription (1)	Special general increase (2)	1st, 2nd, 3rd general replenishment (3)	Fourth general replenishment (4)	Cumulative approved loans	Cumulative disbursement
1974	15	80,659	80,659	—	—	—	41,999	—
1975	17	132,902	99,659	33,243	—	—	125,680	3,492
1976	18	305,902	113,159	33,243	159,500	—	197,630	13,072
1977	20	398,929	128,123	45,579	225,227	—	325,145	36,828
1978	20	407,929	128,123	45,579	234,227	—	430,215	73,258
1979	22	950,018	134,623	45,579	769,816	—	668,366	120,194
1980	23	1,134,018	144,623	45,579	943,816	—	900,536	202,290
1981	24	1,167,018	159,623	45,579	961,816	—	1,190,756	288,748
1982	26	1,761,538	173,623	45,579	1,542,336	—	1,543,328	411,165
1983	26	2,219,891	173,623	45,579	2,000,689	—	1,899,873	575,622
1984	26	2,274,911	173,623	45,579	2,055,709	—	2,308,835	700,460
1985	27	3,409,301	188,623	45,579	2,063,329	1,111,770	2,743,021	914,180
1986	27	3,808,629	188,623	45,579	2,063,329	1,511,098	3,263,256	1,164,256

Note: A fifth replenishment has been successfully negotiated for 1988-90. The replenishment is for $2.7 billion, an increase of $1 billion over the fourth replenishment. Source: African Development Bank Planning and Research Department, *Compendium of Statistics* (1984, 1987).

tries. The funds have amounted to Units of Account (UA) 11.1 million and UA 0.9 million, respectively. These special trust funds have provided less financial resources than originally anticipated.

Prior to 1982 the major problem of the Bank was the scarcity of economic resources for a continent with unlimited economic needs. Since 1982, ironically, the augmentation of resources described above has not been followed by the funding of the proportionate level of new projects for several reasons. First, many of the poorest countries cannot qualify for ADB funding; they are only eligible for precious and scarce concessionary funds. Second, many of the same African members have been in arrears both on payments of subscriptions and on repayments of outstanding loans. As described in detail in chapter 5, sanctions for arrears may mean ongoing projects are stopped and plans for new projects are scrapped. Third, projects reviewed by the governing body, the executive board, have come under close scrutiny for their technical viability. Loans take a longer time for approval, although the quality of the projects passed are higher. What this means is that the ADB group has substantial economic resources, but they may not be the right "mix" between conventional and concessionary resources or be disbursed in a rapid and timely fashion.

The ADB group does possess unique political resources, although in several cases the political resources may also turn into liabilities. First, the ADB at its founding was established as an exclusively African institution. Non-African members were explicitly rejected from participation, the founders extolling the virtues of "going it alone." Not only was all Bank management African, including the president, executive directors, and staff, but donors were exclusively African—a provision severely limiting available economic resources. The restriction against extraregional participation was modified with the establishment of the African Development Fund, facilitating extraregional contributions, and later with the opening up in 1982 of Bank capital to extraregionals. This critical change in membership occurred following extensive negotiations between the regionals and extraregionals (see chapter 4 for details). The principal compromises included an increase in the number of members on the executive board and guarantees of both a two-to-one ratio between regional and extraregional members and for an African president and regular staff.

This guarantee of "Africanicity" in the Bank has been very important symbolically, an outward manifestation of the members' intense desire to rid themselves of neocolonialism. As the Libyan executive director stated, "Whenever possible, we want to maintain our African identity. This is our strength. We feel that speaking as an African to an African is better than if you send a Dutchman or a German to talk to an African" (quoted in Thurow 1989:11). As became evident during the negotiations leading to the admission of the extraregionals in the late 1970s, participants did not agree on what precisely preservation of the African character of the Bank entailed. As ADB President Ford-wor described,

It was quite obvious that not everyone understood the term in the same way. For some, the idea was a purely political and historical concept. The bank was an expression of African determination to help itself and to demonstrate that it was free of its colonial-period dependence on non-African and largely imperialistic economic influences. For those of this view, to open up the bank was precisely to admit that it was impossible to give concrete expression to this determination in economic terms. For them it was a total negation of a passionately held ideology which had inspired and sustained many of them through several years of often violent anticolonial conflict. [1981:116]

Africanicity may be viewed as a political resource in another way. The ADB was recognized as the "best" African international organization quite early. Using data collected for the years between 1964 and 1970, John F. Clark (1979:343) found that the ADB received the highest rating by the African states themselves, while the Organization of African Unity (OAU) and the United Nations' Economic Commission for Africa (ECA) followed. Some have suggested that this political distinction may be of dubious advantage, given the relatively poor reputation and ineffectiveness of other continental African organizations. Yet the ADB has only recently been in the financial position to capitalize on its reputation. In 1989 the Bank was heralded as that "rarest of African species: a success" (Thurow, 1989:1).

The African ties have also proved a liability. States in arrears are more likely to approach their African "brothers" seeking time extensions for nonpayment because Africans "understand" the difficult situation. As one ADB official reported, "One head of state who was in arrears on a project told my staff, 'You are my brothers, you should understand.' Well, we do understand. We are Africans. But we are also bankers" (quoted in Thurow, 1989:11). Hence, the ADB may be one of the last institutions repaid—a costly price for fraternity. The ADB may be asked to intervene on behalf of African constituents toward other international lending institutions or vice versa. In 1987 when Zambia, refusing to accept proposed reforms, severed relations with the International Monetary Fund (IMF), the ADB not only continued to finance projects but also acted as a go-between with that country's creditors. Many contend that ADB should provide a "softening" cushion against harsh IMF-imposed conditionalities.

A second political resource on which the African Development Bank group can capitalize is the presence of a weighted voting arrangement, which while permitting those who have contributed most to have a greater voice in governance, is relatively egalitarian compared to the other multilateral development banks. At the establishment of the Bank, votes were allocated to African states according to a formula that tended to equalize influence. For example, basic votes, those allocated equally to each member whether a Nigeria or a Togo, accounted for one-half of the total. When votes were added according to the amount of subscriptions, the ratio between the country with the largest number of votes and the smallest was 5 to 1, even though the maximum ratio of subscriptions was 30 to 1 (Krasner, 1981). This was pecularily egalitarian because Bank decisions were taken by a simple majority vote. In a continent of countries so concerned with state identify, this semblance of equality, unusual for a financial institution, provided legitimacy for the organization.

Concern with the relatively egalitarian voting structure in

the Bank was paramount during the negotiations with the extra-regionals over adhesion. The largest contributors to the Bank—Nigeria, Egypt, the United States, and Japan—obtained only 9.28%, 5.78%, 5.51%, and 4.68%, respectively (ADB/ADF, Board of Governors, *Annual Report* 1986). So it is impossible for any specific country to control voting or exercise veto power—two of the traditional avenues of hegemonic influence. In addition, it was stipulated that regional members control approximately two-thirds of the voting power, with the extraregionals controlling one-third. Changes in rules, as stated in Article 3 of the 1981 revised *Agreement Establishing the African Development Bank*, "may be amended only by decision of the Board of Governors by a two-thirds majority of the total number of governors, including two-thirds of the governors of nonregional [extraregional] members, representing not less than three-fourths of the total voting power of the member countries." Thus, this relatively egalitarian weighted voting system has been an important factor enhancing organizational political legitimacy for the regional members.

In the African Development Fund voting power is equally divided between the African Development Bank (representing one-half) and the extraregional member states. The votes of the extraregional states are allocated in proportion to their share of financial contributions. Yet all major decisions of the Fund require three-fourths approval. Under this arrangement, neither the Bank (representing the less-developed regional members) nor the extraregional members can independently block action. Although this arrangement was designed particularly to preserve the power of the African states, thereby increasing the political legitimacy of the organization for that group, in the case of the Fund, it means that there is little correlation between formal voting power and actual contributions. In the Fund, the Bank, which has one-half of the voting power, has contributed cumulatively only 2.11% of the financial resources through 31 December 1986. Despite this disparity, there does not appear to be much dissatisfaction among the extraregionals. Voting is neither the preferred nor the dominant form of decision making; extraregionals play a more important role than their voting power suggests. The legality of weighted voting ensures legitimacy for the donor countries, but the fact that the "weighting" is equalized and voting is not preferred mode of decision making enhances the legitimacy for African participants and undermines the power of economic or political hegemons.

A third political resource emerges from the ADB policy of working with all types of political regimes. With the exception of South Africa (which is not a member of the organization), ADB's willingness to be virtually "ideology blind" has enhanced the political legitimacy of the institution. The extraregionals have not forced the ADB to alter this policy. For example, although the United States has opposed Bank lending to Ethiopia and Angola, the U.S., with its relatively small percentage of voting power, has been unable to affect ADB's allocation to these two countries. For many African governments, ADB group political legitimacy has been affirmed through this process. As one American official commiserates, because the United States feels guilty about the economic plight of Africa, it wants the ADB to succeed and has not made its demands toward specific regimes too vociferously.

The economic and political resources of the African Development Bank group provide a critical foundation for understanding the patterns of intraorganizational politics (chapter 2). The process the Bank utilizes and the points of political pressure are examined in chapter 3. These processes provide the basis for exploring the policy issues of multinational projects, admission of extraregionals, and agriculture in chapter 4. Chapter 5 examines the techniques that the ADB utilizes to influence borrowing states, and chapter 6, the constraints on that ADB influence. Chapters 7 and 8 assess interorganizational politics between the ADB and other international and national organizations. Chapter 9 describes post hoc evaluation procedures. Finally in chapter 10 the organizational, interorganizational, and hegemonic politics found in the African Development Bank are compared to trends in the World Bank, Inter-American Development Bank, and the Asian Development Bank.

CHAPTER 2

Decision Making within the African Development Bank

At the 1964 founding of the African Development Bank, the wounds of colonialism were too fresh and the desire to be independent too strong to consider Western country membership. ADB members deliberately chose to limit membership and participation to continental countries. Yet what exactly Africanicity meant was never clearly enunciated. At a minimum, members were African states, projects financed would be located in Africa, and African nationals would administer the affairs of the Bank. But as one official present during the early years volunteered, Africanicity did mean something more than "an ideology, born of the hatred of colonialism"; it had pragmatic implications.

How Africanicity was preserved in the working of the organization with the 1982 opening of membership to extraregional states is the subject of this chapter. The focus is on the ADB as an institution: how the various organs in the organization actually operate. Intraorganizational politics is both a cooperative and conflictual process.

One of the persistent themes of African politics is personal leadership, rule by a person imbued with a host of both formal and informal powers, ideally possessing traditional and modern legitimacy (Jackson and Rosberg 1982). Leadership within the African Development Bank, centered in the president, is no exception. While the president is elected by the board of governors on the recommendation to the board of directors (ADB 1981a, Art. 26), it is the president who has "the highest competence in matters pertaining to the activities, management and administration of the Bank" (Art. 36). And according to Article 7, it is the president who shall be for a five-year period chairman of the board of directors (with power of voting only in tie), the chief of staff of the Bank, and the Bank's chief legal representative. Beyond these formal powers, the president, like executive heads of IGOs generally, has informal responsibilities: to establish the programmatic agenda, to determine speed of organizational change, and to legitimate the activities of the Bank in the international community. Hence, given both the formal legal powers of the office, as well as the informal powers accrued, it is not surprising to find that election for the position is a highly contentious process.

Unlike some of the other multilateral development banks which have both constitutionally mandated stipulations or strong precedents that the president come from a certain country (for example, World Bank, an American; Asian Development Bank, a Japanese), members of the African Development Bank ask that the president be African. With the large number of independent African states, the number of contenders has been large. In the words of one official, it takes almost a year before the election for the list of candidates to dwindle to a manageable number. During that time, programmatic activity grinds to a halt "as jockeying among the candidates" to get in the "right position" and to obtain support from the "right states" becomes a full-time occupation. The controversy involves not only the professional suitability of one candidate over another, but perhaps more importantly their potential "representativeness," linguistically whether they are anglophone, francophone, or Arab-speaking, and geographically whether they are from the east, west, north, or south.

This divisiveness can be best illustrated by examination of the presidential election records. For example during the May 1975 board of governors' meeting, five candidates originally presented themselves: D. Bihute (Burundi), G.O. Onosode

(Nigeria), A. Laraki (Morocco), K.D. Fordwor (Ghana), and S. Omeish (Libya). Eventually the first three candidates withdrew. On the first ballot, Fordwor received 43.98% of the vote from twenty-three countries and Omeish received 45.10% from only fourteen countries, with Nigeria (7.86%) abstaining. Among all the countries supporting specific officials, only one logical pattern is evident. The North African countries, three of whom wield an especially large vote (Algeria, 7.40%; Egypt, 6.58%; and Libya, 7.31%), and to a lesser extent Tunisia and Morocco all voted for the Libyan candidate. A second ballot was held in which precisely the same country votes were tallied, including the abstentions. Without a victor, an agreement was hammered out extending the term of then-President Abdelwahab Labidi for another year.

These proceedings were peppered with innuendos and suggestions about the appropriate procedures for presidential elections. For example, Zambia proposed a regional rotation system to prevent one region from exerting undue control over the others (singling out "our Arab brothers"). Others sought much more informal discussions before actual votes were taken. Still others voiced disgust with the procedures actually followed. Changing the rules in midst of the election and engaging in bloc voting were political behaviors unbecoming and inappropriate for a bank. The public disgust expressed concerning this infighting for the presidency suggests that both the rules had not yet become formally institutionalized and that states were operating under the illusion that the election could be conducted apolitically.

In 1976 Fordwor was elected president after months of political maneuvering. He won 50.66% of the votes, compared to 35.77% and 6.44% for his two opponents, and 6.03% abstentions (Fordwor 1981:55). This time the board of governors acted alone, seemingly without the nomination of the executive directors, a procedure at variance with the intent of the founding agreements. Following the election, there was considerable commentary on the appropriateness of bloc voting. Some states, including Guinea and Ghana, argued forcefully that consideration of such factors as language, regional origin, and pigmentation in voting for the president are but permanent reminders of colonialist tactics to divide and exploit Africans. But recognition of this divisiveness did not lead to changed behavior. Four years later (following "l'affaire Fordwor" discussed below), the presidential election was again conducted on the basis of "parochialism and language divisions."

The controversy surrounding President Fordwor almost led to the demise of the ADB as an institution. Fordwor's book (1981) offers his interpretation of the events. The purpose in reviewing the events is to substantiate that political in-fighting and maneuvering has occurred periodically even before the extraregionals joined, lending support to the thesis that the ADB was a political institution even without Western economic hegemon's membership.

The notes from the board of governors' meetings in 1979 and 1980, together with the memorandum between Fordwor and the board, show overt political conflict. At the 1979 regular meeting of the board of governors held in Abidjan, 14-18 May, President Fordwor was lauded for his negotiations with the extraregionals for admission; there was no manifest indication that Fordwor's performance as president was viewed as unacceptable. Shortly thereafter (on 1 June), President Fordwor received a letter from the executive directors denouncing many of his decisions, including his opening of regional offices in London, Washington, D.C., and Nairobi; appointment of personnel; changing of financial regulations; conducting secret discussions with the board of governors; and mismanagement of the electoral process in the executive board. These charges all revolve around the executive board's assertion that the president was making unilateral decisions without thorough and constitutionally mandated consultation with the executive directors. Fordwor was accused of being the major "player" in the ADB, not the neutral participant envisaged by economic technocrats.

On 19 June 1979, Fordwor responded in detail to these accusations. He denied taking any measures to exclude the executive directors from decision making. His conception was that executive directors were responsible for the overall direction of policy, but that the president made daily policy and personnel decisions. Such decisions were clearly within the president's prerogative.

As the controversy continued, the accusations from both the executive directors and Fordwor grew more bitter. Fordwor was accused of mismanagement, hiring too many fellow Ghanaians and of negotiating an unauthorized $1.5 million contract with Harvard University without consulting the executive directors. In an extraordinary meeting of 25 June, a resolution was passed for Fordwor to cease performing his functions as president. Over the next several days, discussions focused on the legality of the executive directors' action, with Fordwor trying to outmaneuver the board by refusing to call meetings. On 18 June Resolution No. 79 passed terminating Fordwor's position and affirming to the board of governors the action that had been taken. President Goodall Gondwe replaced Fordwor.

This bitter controversy undermined the ADB as an institution. The political powers of the executive directors, the president, and the board of governors were all called into question. The aftermath of bitter feelings among the major antagonists continued to influence organizational processes until the mid-1980s. As most interviewees acknowledge, the institution was on the brink of dismantling itself.

Despite the experience of the Fordwor controversy and Nigeria's sage warnings that the presidential system had resulted in unnecessary, even dangerous "inter-African rivalry" and "confusion," politiking for the position in 1980 was equally as intense. Five candidates mustered enough support to get on the first ballot: A. Sall of Senegal, D. Bihute of Burundi, W. Mungomba of Zambia, D.S. Sylla of Mali, and T. Sangare of Guinea. Four ballots were necessary before a president was elected. To a large extent, analysis of the voting suggests that "friends and neighbors" politics prevailed. For example, on the first ballot, the Senegalese candidate was supported by Senegal, Gambia, and Cameroon; the Burundi candidate by his native country and neighboring Rwanda, Uganda, and Zaire; the Zambian candidate by Zambia, Zimbabwe, Swaziland, and Lesotho; and the Guinean candidate by a number of west African neighbors including Benin, Ivory Coast, Liberia, Sierra Leone, and Togo.

These patterns do not, of course, tell the whole story, because eleven countries or 16.80% of the voters abstained, including such subregional powers as Angola, Ethiopia, Ghana, Kenya, and Tanzania.

On the second and third ballot, Sangare, Sylla, and Mung-omba remained in contention. On the second ballot the abstentions still played a critical role, representing 20.07% of the vote. By the third ballot, Ethiopia, Kenya, and Tanzania rallied around Mung-omba, giving him support from eighteen countries and 46.23% of the vote; Ghana supported Sangare (24.94% from sixteen countries); and Angola, for Sylla (16.53% from fourteen countries). On the fourth ballot, although abstentions still comprised 13.42% of the votes, Mung-omba received 50.37% of the votes from nineteen countries, compared to Sangare's 35.21% from nineteen countries. These elections illustrate that the weighted voting system, even though the between-country differentials were relatively small, did make a difference. The more powerful countries played a crucial role in the presidential elections.

Dissatisfaction with presidential politiking finally resulted in some procedural changes in the 1985 election for president. Voting was secret for the first time. The results were reported in summary fashion. The three candidates P. C. Damiba (Burkina Faso), D. Mung-omba (Zambia), and Babacar N'Diaye (Senegal) vied during two ballots; only percentages and regional/extraregional breakdowns were given. On the first ballot, 17.19% were in abstention of which 14% were the extraregionals; support by the regional members was about equally divided between Mung-omba and N'Diaye (22% for each). By the second ballot, there were virtually no abstentions, and N'Diaye had mustered 63.39%, compared to 27.48% for Mung'omba and Damiba's 6.72%. The real strength of N'Diaye's position came from the extraregionals, who seemed to unite behind the candidate, whereas the regional members gave 36.82% of their vote to the winner. Country votes were never reported.

With the 1985 secret-ballot election, rivalries among the African members were muted. A new political variable entered into the calculation—the position of the donor extraregional members. This combination of factors, however, including the unfortunate Fordwor controversy, the dissatisfaction with voting according to regional or linguistic criteria, the entrance of the extraregionals into the organization and the secret ballot, has made the presidential contest less overtly controversial. Responsibility for this turn of events goes to the candidate finally selected in 1985—Babacar N'Diaye—in the words of one "a son of the bank."

President N'Diaye has been on the Bank's professional staff since 1965. In his previous position as vice president of finance, he engineered the Bank's bid to earn a top credit rating and developed close ties with the international banking community. Given the substantial power the president wields, jockeying for the position is likely to be a permanent feature of the ADB institution. But interviewees anticipate that with a "professional president" elected, political conflict in the office will diminish. Yet any president must win election (or reelection)—hence they must conduct what Fordwor describes as a "continental electioneering campaign" (1981:18).

The president sets the overall tone of the organization. The individual is also the administrator for the large international secretariat headquartered in Abidjan, Ivory Coast. This organization has been both described as employing "some of the best and brightest minds on the continent" and only emulating other international secretariats, where "political more than economic" factors prevail, "where people come from still makes a big difference" (Thurow, 1989:1). As true as both perspectives may be, an examination of the changes that have occurred within the secretariat over time suggests increasing professionalization and specialization and decreasing political conflict.

Two of the problems discussed at the second meeting of the board of directors in 1965 are indicative of the difficulties in establishing an international secretariat from *terra incognita*. First, with respect to the election of a vice president, many averred that there should be multiple vice presidents "representing" the different regions. Yet the first vice president did not even present himself in Abidjan until five months after election. Second, the Ivory Coast as host state was soundly criticized for not providing temporary headquarters, for not remodeling a building suitable for the interim, and for constructing a new building out of state funds. The delegates even passed a resolution that the Ivorian government should build houses for the Bank's staff or provide houses with restricted rents.

Compared to the "high expectations" of the founders, the resources available to the secretariat were nominal. Resources were too meager to finance the residence of twelve executive directors and secretariat staff in Abidjan. Executive directors' salaries were $20,000 (even though all held other jobs), and in addition they received a $4,000 personal allowance, a housing allowance, $40 per diem for time in Abidjan, and a $100 monthly expense allowance each. Although the housing allowance was unspecified, a study reported that during 1965 a "house suitable for a director" in Abidjan rented for $1000 a month. The salaries of executive directors and their alternates and the president would consume approximately one-half of what the Bank earned from its capital. This did not include staff assistance and technical personnel in the nascent secretariat. During these initial meetings, not a single development project was submitted. Hence, it is not surprising that grumbles of executive directors and secretariat greed circulated among members of the international banking community.

By the end of 1965 the staff of the Bank numbered forty-five, an increase of thirty-two working during the first year. As resources have increased and as the secretariat has taken over specialized activities, the staffing has increased exponentially. Gardiner and Pickett (1984:36) report that by the end of 1976, 322 worked in the secretariat, one-third of which were classified as professionals. By the end of 1986, the staff reached 966, 40.3% of whom are professionals, 5.2% subprofessionals, 42.7% general services, and 11.8% manual workers (ADB/ADF, Board of Governors, *Annual Report* 1986:79). Included among the vice presidents is the first American, Milan Kerno. Approximately 5 or 6% of the staff are nationals from extraregional members. The seven to ten Americans employed by 1986 include the vice president and experts in health and education, demography, finance, and translation (U.S. House of Representatives, 1986).

The reputation of the secretariat has only slowly changed from the negative image of the 1960s. The highly visible "presidential politics" game described earlier has been one reason why the image stuck. Fordwor described the working climate of the secretariat as late as 1977 as polarized with petty jealousy and rivalry. Morale was low during the Fordwor affair. Many of the more qualified Africans were employed by the major international financial institutions, including the World Bank and the International Monetary Fund. In these institutions, conditions of employment were vastly superior and professionalization of staff well entrenched.

The negative image of the secretariat and its low morale, symptomatic of that image, has "turned around." By the 1980s the ADB secretariat was attracting academically qualified people, many of whom had diversified "hands-on" experience. "With its pin-striped economists, sophisticated capital-market presentations and no-nonsense attitude, the bank has given the business world a new picture of Africa" (Thurow, 1989:1). Now the secretariat has been described by one as composed of "people more qualified than the institution" and in the words of another as a "good staff—weak system."

The administrative organization of the secretariat is relatively simple. As shown on the organization chart in figure 1, the four major units are Operations, Finance, Planning and External Relations, and Administration, each under a vice president. Under Operations, the largest of the units, are four departments—Country Programs, Agriculture and Rural Development, Infrastructure and Industry, and Central Projects Unit—and the regional offices. The regional offices have been part of an effort to decentralize operations, although the success of decentralization is questionable. Under Finance are the Treasury and Accounts departments. Three departments are encompassed in the Planning and External Relations, including Planning and Research, Cooperation, and Training Center. And finally, under Administration are Personnel and Training, Ad-

Figure 1. Organization of the African Development Bank

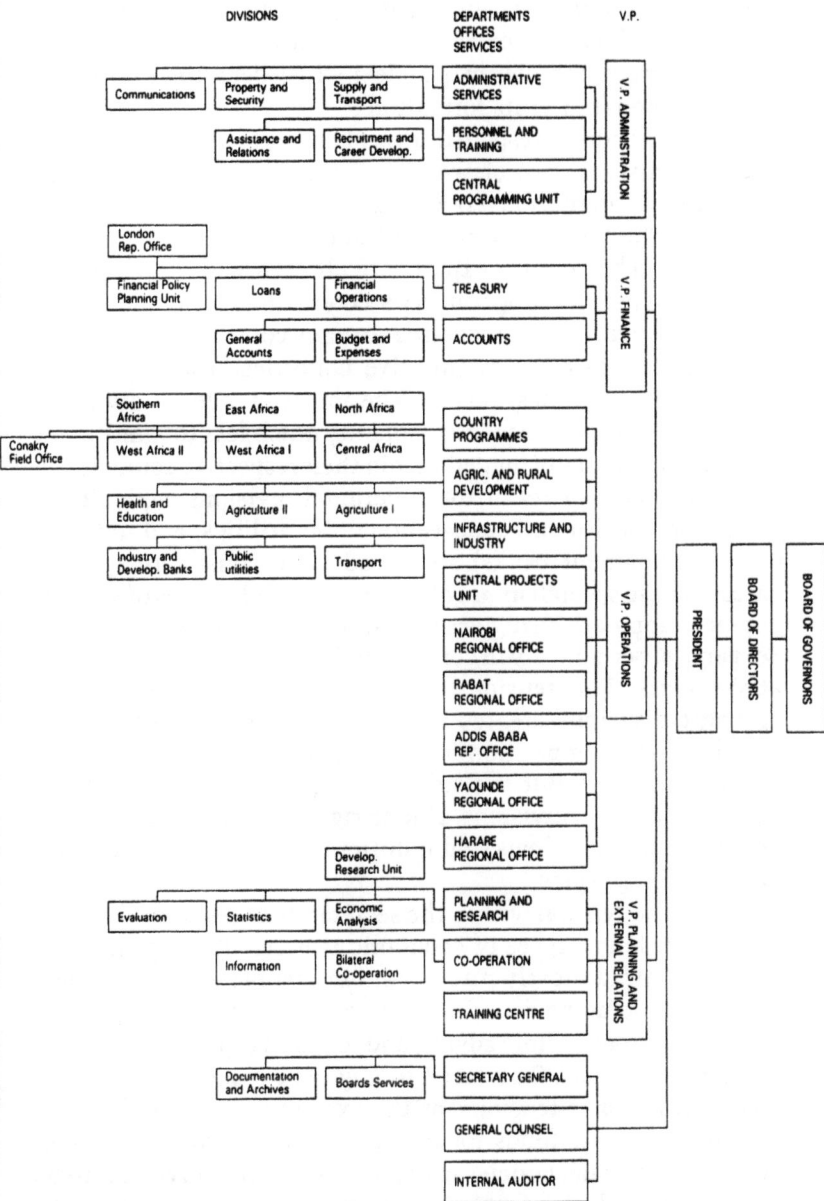

DIVISIONS | DEPARTMENTS OFFICES SERVICES | V.P.

V.P. ADMINISTRATION
- ADMINISTRATIVE SERVICES — Communications, Property and Security, Supply and Transport
- PERSONNEL AND TRAINING — Assistance and Relations, Recruitment and Career Develop.
- CENTRAL PROGRAMMING UNIT

V.P. FINANCE
- London Rep. Office
- TREASURY — Financial Policy Planning Unit, Loans, Financial Operations
- ACCOUNTS — General Accounts, Budget and Expenses

V.P. OPERATIONS
- Conakry Field Office
- COUNTRY PROGRAMMES — Southern Africa, East Africa, North Africa, West Africa II, West Africa I, Central Africa
- AGRIC. AND RURAL DEVELOPMENT — Health and Education, Agriculture II, Agriculture I
- INFRASTRUCTURE AND INDUSTRY — Industry and Develop. Banks, Public utilities, Transport
- CENTRAL PROJECTS UNIT
- NAIROBI REGIONAL OFFICE
- RABAT REGIONAL OFFICE
- ADDIS ABABA REP. OFFICE
- YAOUNDE REGIONAL OFFICE
- HARARE REGIONAL OFFICE

V.P. PLANNING AND EXTERNAL RELATIONS
- Develop. Research Unit
- PLANNING AND RESEARCH — Evaluation, Statistics, Economic Analysis
- CO-OPERATION — Information, Bilateral Co-operation
- TRAINING CENTRE

- SECRETARY GENERAL — Documentation and Archives, Boards Services
- GENERAL COUNSEL
- INTERNAL AUDITOR

PRESIDENT | BOARD OF DIRECTORS | BOARD OF GOVERNORS

Source: ADB/ADF, Board of Governors, *Annual Report* (1986).

ministrative Services, and Central Programming Unit. This complex and specialized form of organization represents quite a contrast from the eleven people in five departments of the Bank's secretariat at its formation.

This division of responsibilities has led to a number of persistent tensions, two of which are found repeatedly in other specialized international organizations. The first is the tension between the functional divisions and the regional or country divisions. The country experts are charged with developing a holistic approach to a country's economic development, but with so few economists covering so many countries (three country economists cover twenty-five countries), their ability to fulfill the task is questionable. The ability of so few individuals to make valid analytical assessments, much less to monitor all the projects actually funded within their respective countries, is problematic. Experts in the functional divisions (agriculture, transport, health and education, public utilities, and industry and development banks) are called in to consult in specific areas. These specialists are often viewed as advocates of a development approach that gives top priority to their specific area of expertise, periodically in conflict to the views of so-called country experts. This tension between the functional versus geographic divisions creates what some refer to as a "healthy rivalry"—"a competition for resources which results in more sound projects." But it also leads to scrambling for positions between the two divisions. Due to rigidities within the personnel system, individuals find it difficult to move easily between these two divisions.

A second tension within the secretariat arises from the position of different types of economic experts. The organization initially hired mostly microeconomists. Newer approaches, however, including country-wide programming, giving governments macroeconomic advice, and research capabilities require macroeconomists. This need to augment macroeconomic capabilities creates tensions, as the executive directors have refused to allocate funds for new positions. At the same time, current personnel policies make it difficult for individuals to be retrained. Within the secretariat there is a strong perception of a

Table 3. Basic Salary Scales of ADB Secretariat as of October
       1984

Manual Worker	
lowest grade	53,705 CFA* month
highest grade	196,610 CFA month
General Service	
lowest grade	178,692 CFA month (4,624 UA/yr)
highest grade	712,105 CFA month (18,427 UA/yr)
Sub-Professional	
lowest grade	617,271 CFA month (15,973 UA/yr)
highest grade	1,164,827 CFA month (30,142 UA/yr)
Professional	
P category	
lowest grade	785,414 CFA month (20,324 UA/yr)
highest grade	2,214,571, CFA month (57,306 UA/yr)
D category	
lowest grade	2,083,372 CFA month (53,911 UA/yr)
highest grade	2,551,166 CFA month (66,016 UA/yr)

Note: CFA is African franc; 50 CFA = 1 French franc.

system mired in career immobility. Both tensions hinder task
performance and stifle individual initiative.
    Cognizant of these tensions and aware of the need to profes-
sionalize the secretariat, the ADB has been involved in an effort
to institutionalize procedures and personnel policies. The 1981
Staff Manual represents one such effort. Secretariat employees
are categorized as professional, subprofessional, general services, and manual workers, having permanent employment, temporary (six months to five years), and short-term (less than six
months) (ADB, 1981b). Table 3 shows the applicable salary scale
as of October 1984. In addition to the salary, secretariat officials
enjoy a wide range of benefits found in many international
organizations. Officials receive a dependency allowance (for
spouse, legitimate and legally adopted children—specifically
excluded are "adopted" brothers, sisters, cousins, nephews, and
nieces unless legally adopted); an education grant for each child
(UA 1,000 per year for primary or UA 3,000 per year for secondary, or 80% of expenses, including an air ticket if education is

abroad); and an installation allowance for international staff equal to one month's salary or one and one-half months' if accompanied by family. Furthermore the Bank reimburses employees 75% of the cost of all approved medical expenses and contributes to a Provident Fund (7% of wages/salary) to be used for loans to employees. Finally, in addition to an annual leave (vacation), the Bank provides a home leave every two years, paid in full by the Bank.

Despite these internationally competitive rates (especially if benefits are included), secretariat personnel desire a civil service system. Such a system would provide increased opportunity for a career ladder, an expectation that an employee may not only stay in the organization, but that he or she be permitted to advance professionally and change jobs for personal and financial benefit. Most officials express the view that such a system would bolster staff morale. Morale is also a function of external image. And in the eyes of the Abidjan community, ADB secretariat personnel are seen as an "over-paid, privileged and frequently spoiled lot." Frequent abuse of Bank privileges, exemption from local taxes, and ration cards for cheap gasoline exacerbate the poor image and are routinely reported in the daily press of the Ivory Coast *Fraternité-Matin.*

The board of governors is the formal authoritative body of the Bank. This board, composed of one governor and one alternate from each member country, meets once a year in plenary, more often if necessary. This group issues general directives concerning the credit policy of the Bank. Specifically, according to the *Agreement Establishing the African Development Bank,* the governors have exclusive power to authorize the following:

1. Decrease the authorized capital stock of the Bank;
2. Establish or accept the administration of Special Funds;
3. Authorize arrangements for cooperation with African countries which have not yet attained independence;
4. Determine, on recommendation of the Board of Directors, the remuneration and conditions of service of the President of the bank;
5. Determine the remuneration of directors and their alternatives;
6. Certify outside auditors;

7. Approve the General Balance Sheet and Statement of Profit and Loss
   of the Bank. [Chap. V, Art. 29]

A close reading of the minutes of the board of governors meetings suggests that many of these activities are pro forma— the
adoption of the annual report, appointment of external auditors,
and making arrangements for future meetings.

There is substantial evidence, however, that the week-long
meetings can degenerate into political theater, with a variety of
states posturing on issues that are only of nominal or even
remote relevance to the ADB. Based on a perusal of minutes
from the meetings of the board of governors, representatives
from several countries—Libya, Algeria, and Nigeria—have
tended to dominate proceedings. Countries that have recently
joined the Bank also show a higher propensity to dominate the
proceedings, most conspicuously Angola and Zimbabwe during
the 1980 meeting of the board in Abidjan. Discussions among
the governors are highly ideological. For example, Arab-speaking members led by Libya and Algeria have persistently sought
to have Arabic adopted as one of the official languages, either in
addition to English and French or in place of these languages.
These countries were finally successful at getting the *Annual
Report* translated into Arabic and distributed, at a cost reputed
to be seven times greater than that of the other editions.

Although the language controversy has not abated with the
adhesion of the extraregionals to the ADB, the issues debated at
the annual meeting of the board of governors have changed.
Items have been added to the agenda that previously remained
unspoken concerns. For example, the extraregional governors
have indicated the need for comprehensive country programming, more monitoring of loans to improve overall quality, and a
speeding up of loan disbursement. Recruitment of extraregional
staff to the secretariat and the Bank's sensitivity to the role of
women in economic development are two current issues of
concern to extraregional governors. In other words, the board of
governors has become a more issue-oriented forum since the
arrival of the extraregionals. High-ranking officials from mem-

ber countries, often the finance ministers, increasingly use the forum of the board of governors to pose some difficult questions and chart new directions for the Bank.

Decision making in the board of governors is by the weighted voting system, each member having 625 votes, in addition to one vote for each share of the capital stock of the Bank held by that member. According to Article 35 of the *Agreement Establishing the African Development Bank,* each delegate is entitled to cast the number of votes he represents, with matters being decided by majority. In practice, few of the issues discussed at board of governors' meetings are settled by this voting procedure. With consensus decision making the norm in the board of governors, political controversy is more apparent within the board of directors.

The executive directors are entrusted with the responsibility of charting the general operations of the Bank. This group, in addition to exercising all the powers delegated to it by the board of governors, is responsible for the following tasks:

1. Appointing one or more Vice Presidents of the Bank, on recommendation of the President;
2. Preparing the work of the Board of Governors;
3. Making decisions concerning particular direct loans, guarantees, investments in equity capital and borrowing of funds by the Bank, in conformity with the general directives of the Board of Governors;
4. Determining the rates of interest for direct loans and of commissions for guarantees;
5. Submitting the accounts for each financial year and an annual report for approval to the Board of Governors;
6. Determining the general structure of the services of the Bank. [ABD 1981a, Art. 32]

Until May 1982 the executive directors numbered nine, elected by the board of governors and grouped to represent various African constituencies. With the admission of the extraregionals, there are eighteen executive directors, twelve members from the regional countries and six from the extraregionals. A discussion of the controversy surrounding this increase is cataloged in chapter 4. These directors and their alternates are charged with representing a specific group of states, or in one case, one state. They receive their compensation and allowances from the African Development Bank, an arrangement that presumably gives the directors more economic independence to represent constituent interests. The one exception to this financial arrangement is the case of the American director, the only director representing a single state. His or her salary is paid by the Bank to the U.S. Department of the Treasury, which in turn remunerates the director in accord with the wage rate of the Treasury Department. This system prevents the American director from being paid more than his Washington colleagues, even if it does mean that he is being paid less than his fellow directors in Abidjan.

The following eighteen groups are organized in the board of executive directors:

Regional Representatives:
 1. Guinea, Morocco, Togo, Tunisia
 2. Ghana, Gambia, Liberia, Sierra Leone
 3. Angola, Botswana, Mozambique, Zimbabwe
 4. Djibouti, Egypt
 5. Lesotho, Malawi, Mauritius, Swaziland, Zambia
 6. Chad, Cape Verde, Somalia, Sudan, Zaire
 7. Burundi, Central African Republic, Comoros, Gabon, Mali, Senegal
 8. Ethiopia, Kenya, Uganda, Rwanda, Seychelles, Tanzania
 9. Benin, Burkina Faso, Cameroon, Congo, Ivory Coast, Equatorial Guinea, Niger
10. Libya, Mauritania
11. Algeria, Guinea Bissau, Madagascar
12. Nigeria, Sao-Tomé and Principe

Extraregional Representatives:
13. Federal Republic of Germany, The Netherlands, Portugal, United Kingdom
14. Belgium, France, Italy
15. Denmark, Finland, India, Norway, Sweden, Switzerland
16. Canada, South Korea, Kuwait, Spain, Yugoslavia
17. Austria, Saudi Arabia, Brazil, Japan
18. United States

An examination of these various groups of executive directors suggests that many groups are based upon a combination of geographic propinquity and in the African case, linguistic preference. The extraregional groupings represent a haphazard agglomeration of states put together for a variety of reasons. Most critical to the functioning of the executive directors is the voting ratio: two-thirds of votes for the regionals and one-third for the extraregionals. In the actual meetings of the executive directors, however, votes are seldom taken. Voting on projects is often by resolution, with countries likely to express their disapproval by abstention. By the time a project has reached the board, the resolution is more a formality.

The United States executive director is a unique case. He is unique in the level of consultation conducted with the home office. All loans proposed by the ADB are sent to Washington, D.C., to be evaluated by the Working Group on Multilateral Assistance, a group headed by Treasury Department officials with members from the Departments of State, Commerce, and the U.S. Agency for International Development (USAID). This group assesses all loans proposed in all the multilateral development banks on the basis of whether they are consistent with general American foreign policy guidelines, as well as whether the projects as properly conceived. No other executive director receives a comparable amount of input or, indeed, actual policy directives from his home ministry. The American executive director is, as a result, more informally circumscribed by his country's domestic politics than the other executive directors are.

Until the 1980s, all the American executive directors sent to the African Development Bank were political appointees, and admittedly in the words of both ADB secretariat and American officials themselves, not always of the highest quality. The use of political appointees may be one explanation of the devolution of power back to the Treasury Department itself. Professional Treasury Department officials of late occupy the executive director position, personnel who have worked in similar capacities with other regional development banks and with the project evaluating unit. These professionals see themselves as both advocates of the Bank *and* representatives of the United States.

They argue that the United States wants to approve ADB loans; they justify the lengthy evaluation process as necessary to improve the quality of proposals.

When the United States has questioned ADB loans, it has been through the executive director. Compared to the American position in the other development banks such as the World Bank and Inter-American Dvelopment Bank, the United States has not consistently acted to tie up or vote against loans for political reasons. Two exceptions to this generalization continue to occur. Under the Gonzalez Amendment the United States may not approve loans to countries that have unfairly expropriated property of American citizens or corporations. The Reagan administration has used this amendment consistently to oppose ADB loans to Ethiopia. According to American officials at the ADB, use of the Gonzalez Amendment is an excuse, a justification to oppose loans to the Marxist regime of Ethiopia. These same officials disagree with the use of this legalistic justification, proposing that the United States could oppose such loans for other more palatable reasons, including the flagrant human rights violations in that country. Yet American opposition to the Ethiopian loans has not unduly influenced loan approval: the loans have been passed over American objections. According to ADB officials, the Ethiopian government has one of the best records of disbursement of loans and completion of projects.

Angola is beginning to encounter American opposition to loan requests. Prior to 1985 no loans were requested by Angola. On-going discussions among Angolan and Bank officials are resulting in an ADB pipeline of proposed projects. Although the United States has been politically and ideologically opposed to the Marxist regime in that country, it is unclear whether America will take a more strident stance and try to convince other countries not to support ADB loans. According to both Bank and American officials, the United States will more than likely oppose such loans, but not actively lobby to block passage of the loans.

The case of American opposition at the level of the executive director of the Ethiopian and Angolan cases suggests that the United States will continue to exercise an independent position. Other extraregional directors have not followed America's lead on the Ethiopian or Angolan loans. With no veto power and in many cases having no real political commitment to block the process, the United States has opposed loans without it significantly affecting the institution. This more careful use of American political power in the institution has preserved the perception shared by many in the secretariat and among executive directors that strong American participation is desirable, as long as participation by the economic hegemon in the other multilateral development banks is not abused.

The other extraregional groups operate differently. The Austrian, Saudi Arabian, Brazilian, and Japanese group is essentially dominated by the Japanese. Japan as a large donor always occupies the executive director position, with the alternate position rotating among the other members. The Japanese executive director does receive considerable input from home officials, but consults on a less frequent and more formal way with other members of the group. Obligatory visits are paid to ministry officials, relevant documentation forwarded, and summary statements of the executive directors' meetings and positions submitted. The Canadian, Korean, Kuwait, Spanish, and Yugoslavian group follow much of the same procedures, with Canada as the lead member. But in contrast to Japan, Canada has played a much more active leadership role in the ADB, being instrumental in the establishment of the African Development Fund and convincing France to participate in the whole undertaking.

For the other extraregional groups, the executive directorship is rotated every three years. When one country holds the directorship, the other countries play a markedly passive role in the process. Formal consultation occurs after decisions have been taken. Two reasons for the communication gap are evident. First, administrative bottlenecks often mean that proper documentation is not received in sufficient time to forward it to the various countries before meetings are held and decisions taken. So the director *en place* makes decisions in consultation with his home government. Second, and perhaps more importantly, some of the extraregional members themselves have not taken an active interest in the Bank except when procurement contracts are let. When procurement is at stake, then embassies of extraregionals located in Abidjan often relay the information as quickly as possible so that national firms can bid on procurement contracts.

If consultation by executive directors representing several extraregionals is sporadic, consultation by regional executive directors is even less institutionalized. Several executive directors represent a large number of small states; hence only pro forma ad hoc coordination occurs. In the words of one executive director, most African states only care about getting their own projects passed and receiving their loans. Prior to the admission of the extraregionals, few projects were scrutinized by the directors; both lack of interest by other African states and a shortage of administrators qualified to evaluate projects were responsible for this practice.

With the admission of extraregionals, the orientation of some executive directors changed. Most executive directors from the regional members decide their stance on a pending policy change or a project being proposed and communicate the position to others in the group after the fact. The system operates in part because there are many rotating executive directorships, although the three largest contributors—Libya, Algeria, Nigeria—do tend to hold their positions and their respective country representatives play a conspicuous role in executive directors meetings.

Policy making within the African Development Bank occurs in meetings of the executive directors. Among the executive directors, there is considerable disagreement about the amount of persistent conflict exhibited at these important meetings. Opinions vary from those who see no persistent cleavages in the group (in other words, those who see that personality differences are more controlling than national positions), to those who view a fundamental cleavage between donors and recipients, extraregionals and regionals. Based on the interviews conducted at headquarters and on reading various debates from the executive directors' meetings, there does seem to be a persistent difference in perception among regional and extraregional directors, but these differences are modified by personality and by shifting coalitions based on common positions held by regionals and extraregional members. While a number of these policy issues will be discussed in greater depth in chapters 4 and 5, a general discussion of these different tendencies helps us understand the political dynamics within executive directors' meetings.

At the most basic level, there is a different understanding among the regionals and extraregionals about what groups are critical to national economic development. The regionals put more faith in the state sector, while the extraregionals envisage a process in which the private sector has an important role. Regionals having extensive development plans tend to submit ambitious projects, whereas the extraregionals viewing economic development from a more incremental perspective are skeptical of serial projects in general and of the ability of many African countries to manage such projects. Regionals contend that states should be able to conduct economic development with as little interference from the funding agents as possible, meaning of course, a reticience to accept multilateral advice and formal conditionality. In contrast, the extraregionals argue that a country's overall macroeconomic policy must be scrutinized and advice given, or even conditions imposed, before and during the time that the multilateral funds are spent. And the regionals have traditionally not given much attention to efficiency of management, whereas for the extraregionals developing competent management is essential.

On each of these different questions, there is some overlap in positions among the regionals and extraregionals. For example, the Scandinavians are more tolerant of state sector theories of economic development; and some of the larger African donors, such as Nigeria, are more comfortable with the need to open policy discussions with member governments, even if they do not necessarily desire such discussions for their own government. Personalities certainly do make a difference in softening and hardening positions. The particularly strident personalities of some of the Arab representatives have tended to accentuate the differences between the regionals and extraregionals, whereas the quiet, yet lucid, demeanor of some regional directors has tended to minimize the differences between the regionals and extraregionals. The result is that on many issues there are shifting coalitions in the meetings of the executive directors. These fluid coalitions permit pragmatic interactions with the other parts of the organization, including the board of governors, the president, and the secretariat.

The work load of the executive board has been increasingly relegated to committees, even though many of these meet as committees of the whole. The committees include Finance, Operations, Administration, Surveillance, and Personnel. The committee system has been controversial. The regionals insist that the same two-thirds/one-third regional/extraregional ratio be preserved on all committees, including the politically sensitive audit committee. With work being parceled out to committees, the executive directors are less likely to follow the traditional attitude described by one informant "c'est ça."

This discussion has focused on the patterns of decision making only within the African Development Bank. In fact, the ADB group consists of several units. In 1964 the African Development Bank was established with only African members. In 1972, in accord with Article 8 of the Bank's charter, the African Development Fund was established. As stated earlier, the resources from this fund are designed to be used for concessional lending. Funds are generated by initial subscription by the Bank and thirteen other signatories to the African Development Fund Charter, extraregional participants. The mechanics of this arrangement are described by Gardiner and Pickett:

There is a Board of Governors in whom all powers of the Fund are vested. Its members are elected by the Bank and State participants. There is also a Board of Directors responsible for the general operations of the Fund. It comprises 12 Directors, of whom 6 (and their alternates) are appointed by the State participants, and the other 6 (and their alternates) by the Bank. The Directors hold office for a period of three years and serve without payment from the Fund. The President of the African Development Bank is ultimately responsible for the Fund's operations, including the preparation of an annual budget and the lending programme. The Fund does not have an administrative structure of its own. It uses the offices, staff, organization, services and facilities of the Bank and reimburses it a reasonable proportion of administrative expenses in respect of operations undertaken on behalf of the Fund. [1984:30]

Hence, the African Development Bank and the African Development Fund are separate legal entities but they share structures. Despite the legal anomalies of this relationship (Mvioki, 1985; Wodie, 1984), most practitioners contend that this distinction is both useful and workable. When executive directors meet, they consider both ADB and ADF projects, wearing two hats, employing different criteria depending on the source of the funding. Although administratively the two types of loans pass through the same process, accounting is kept separate for each type of lending and then aggregated for the African Development Bank group reports.

The Nigerian Trust Fund (NTF) is the third institution of the Bank group, coming into force in April 1976. Based on the models of both the African Development Fund and the Venezuelan Trust Fund of the Inter-American Development Bank, Nigeria agreed to contribute additional resources for concessionary funding (at the outset Naira 60 million). In accord with Article 1 of the *Agreement Between the Federal Republic of Nigeria and the African Development Bank for the Establishment of the Nigerian Trust Fund*, "The purpose of the Fund shall be to enable Nigeria to make an increasingly effective contribution to the economic development and social progress of Africa, especially of those member countries of the Bank which are relatively less developed or are most seriously affected by unpredictable catastrophies, including adverse international economic events, through the financing of projects which will further economic and social development in their territories." The Bank manages the Fund, in accord with its regular procedures, but is obligated to consult regularly with Nigeria's governor and obtain Nigerian agreement on the pipeline of projects. When practicable, Nigerian consultants are to be used for carrying out studies. The Trust Fund has not had the impact envisioned. Other of the more economically advantaged regional members have not followed Nigeria's lead in establishing trust funds, and due to its precarious economic situation following the decline in petroleum prices, Nigeria itself has been slow to replenish the fund. Nigeria announced in May 1981 that replenishment would be Naira 50 million; 35 million was paid in 1981 and 8 million in May 1985. With this amount, twenty-eight loans have been granted from the NFT, but only five in 1986 and one in 1985, principally because so many countries are in arrears and cannot obtain new nonconcessional loans.

The divided decision-making structures found in the ADB group, similar to those found in other international economic organizations, provide ample opportunities for various constituencies to express different views and exercise overlapping authority. The ambiguous legal distribution of authority among the president, the executive directors, and the board of governors, surfaced during "l'affaire Fordwor." The settling of that crisis has provided some clarification of responsibilities, although the presidency remains a critically important and powerful office. With the adhesion of the extraregionals, the electoral process for the president has been modified and conflict more subdued. With extraregional membership, however, the board of governors has become more active and the executive directors more politically controversial. In the former case, governors now engage in substantive policy debates; in the latter case, directors give closer scrutiny to the quality of the work of the ADB secretariat and to the proposals and implementation of projects by state authorities. Although differences between regionals and extraregionals do persist as expected, the political cleavages since 1982 have not effectively blocked the lending process.

The Lending Process

The process employed by the institutional actors described in chapter 2 leads to a loan and concludes with a completed project. This process has undergone continual revision. In the Bank's early years, because of the small number of technical staff and the staff's conception of the appropriate procedures for a development bank, Bank officials waited until a member government approached the ADB with a project. Loan applications came slowly, but once received, they were quickly passed through the various procedures, and the loan was usually approved. Appraisal was prefunctory; presentation of the loan to the executive board resulted in virtually automatic funding. And ADB monitoring of implementation was minimal. This nondirective approach to allocating and administering funds began to change in the late 1970s.

In the mid-1970s the secretariat hired Price Waterhouse Associates to conduct a management study of the ADB. The 1977 report elucidated a number of difficulties with the loose administrative process and proposed specific changes. This investigation of the weaknesses in the administrative process had far-reaching consequences. In the revealing words of one participant, the ADB rules were too lax and changed too frequently, so even earnest personnel were lost in the bureaucratic maze.

One of the outcomes of this evaluation was the mandate to write a manual of operating procedures in which the steps in the loan process would be specified and the appropriate form for reports would be outlined. In preparing this manual, ADB personnel were sent to the World Bank as well as to the other regional banks to compare procedures and processes. By 1984 a two-volume *Manual of Operating Procedures* (ADB, 1984d) was circulated in draft form, describing the responsibilities and administrative tasks to ensure a standardized approach.

The *Manual* has received mixed reviews. Officials from co-financing institutions like the World Bank see this institutionalization of procedures and process as a positive development. Even though procedures are always subject to periodic reevaluation and change, the *Manual* permits an "outsider" to follow the entire process. In contrast, a number of those working within the ADB itself scoff at the *Manual*, relegating it to the back shelf of the bookcase. This attitude reflects the position that such a handbook could never accurately record the intricate and sensitive procedures of negotiations; for others, such a manual represents an unwanted intrusion and monitoring of their professional responsibilities. Such attitudes condition receptivity to the manual and the standardization it implies. The formal process as described in the *Manual* and gleaned from interviews with participants is examined below. Understanding the institutional procedures, including the points where ADB personnel and member governments bargain and negotiate for funds, permits us to identify specific steps where political factors or controversies may intervene in the process.

Projects originate from diverse sources. According to the *Manual*, the ADB waits until it receives from member government authorities a request for a loan. The ADB is presented a proposal outlining the nature of the project and its economic, technical, and financial viability. In actuality, the idea for the project may have been mutually negotiated between officials of any one or several of the international lending institutions, including collaboration with a resident representative from the World Bank and member government officials. ADB officials are not resident in any country, but periodic missions sent on other projects often work in conjunction with government officials to develop new projects. In short, the model of the development bank as "autonomous receiver" of projects, while compatible with a view of the MDBs as economically neutral, is too simplistic.

Some ideas for projects do, indeed, arrive at headquarters in this form; others have already been the subject of intense discussion between the ADB (and other cofinancing institutions) and member governments before they appear at headquarters. And many proposals do not arrive at headquarters as a project. Countries may think they have a project and yet not have completed the necessary preinvestment survey.

Projects may also originate as a result of other projects. With country programming, officials identify sector priorities and specific projects that might provide critical linkages for the country's economic development program. The country report (often compiled by one or two economists, following a two-week visit to the country) presents general economic data about the country. Based on the country's announced economic priorities and the Bank's sectoral lending program, the Bank develops the country program including a project pipeline for the upcoming three to four years. That process worked smoothly for the preparation of ADB's 1985 report on Ethiopia (ADB, 1985b). Consistent with sectoral priorities, ADB projects should concentrate on small farms and small-scale irrigation. The process was less helpful for the Comoros (ADB, 1984c). The author of that report had difficulty determining government priorities in the absence of any national development plans since 1978.

The country programming approach to project identification is viewed as a weak link in the ADB process. Too few projects are identified in this manner; few officials make the necessary linkages at the project identification stage. Headquarter personnel often do not have up-to-date and accurate economic information on the country. Perhaps most important, the country programming approach has the potential to be politically explosive. ADB officials carefully avoid attributing the cause of a nation's economic problems to government policy; however, the country programming approach often implicates the governments in failing to develop linkages among economic development projects.

Once a project has been proposed to ADB authorities—a "decision to pursue the project examination"—and if sufficient funds are available, a feasibility study is conducted from external technical assistance funds. The project is then placed in the country's pipeline. The pipeline is a list of projects, prioritized by the government, that the ADB might consider funding. Approximately 40% of the projects in the pipeline are eventually dropped by the government, usually because of an alteration in government priorities or because they have been "picked up" (i.e., funded) by another agency. At this point because the ADB has made no significant investment in the project, there is no objection to deleting projects from the pipeline.

In the next phase, the ADB recommends the project for appraisal. An appraisal team of several ADB officials (including ideally at minimum a technical expert and an economist) journey to the country to visit with government officials and gather data in preparation for the appraisal report. The task of the ADB appraisal is to assess the technical and economic viability of the project and update the prospects for the project. To the Bank (Gardiner and Pickett, 1984:71), technical viability means that the methods chosen for the project and the project itself be appropriate to the conditions for which they are intended. Increasingly, independent contractors or consultants are hired to evaluate the technical specifications. The methods used to calculate financial and economic viability for the appraisal report are standardized, but there is disagreement among officials on their suitability to the task and their applicability. As Gardiner and Pickett explain, "Financial and economic viability mean simply that projects and programmes should be profitable— that is that when all capital and other costs have been fully met there should be a surplus. The difference between the two is a matter of pricing. In financial calculations, inputs and outputs are valued at whatever prices imperfect markets, government controls and other 'distortions' throw up. Against this, economic calculation requires that 'real' opportunity cost or scarcity values in the economy should be used" (1984:71).

An examination of appraisal reports shows that the indicator most often cited is the economic rate of return, calculated on the basis of initial expense, recurrent expenses to ensure operating conditions, and growth, compared to benefits (ADF, *Appraisal Report. Panganales Canal Development Project, Demo-*

cratic Republic of Madagascar, 1983; ADB, *Appraisal Report,
Serowe-Orapa Road Project, Republic of Botswana,* 1984). In a few
cases, there may have been a sophisticated sensitivity analysis
on the internal rate of return. For example in the ADB, *Appraisal
Report, Botswana Telecommunications III Project* (1981), different conditions were shown to lead to alternative rates of
return. In a few cases, some calculation of a social rate of return
was attempted, as in the ADB, *Appraisal Report Water Supply in
Cap-Bon Region, Republic of Tunisia* (1983), although the methodology employed was not detailed.

In some cases, no economic rates of return are calculated,
either because multiple projects resulted from a line of credit to
a national development bank (ADB, *Rapport d'Évaluation
Deuzième Ligne de Crédit à la Banque de Dévellopement de
Zambie,* 1980) or because the project was aimed at improving
the performance of a whole sector (ADB, *Appraisal Report
Strengthening of Scientific and Technical Education Project, Republic of Tunisia,* 1984). In a few cases, particularly for ADF
projects, the statistical information may be of such poor quality
that even "guess-estimates" of an economic rate of return are
impossible to make. For example in the ADF's *Appraisal Report,
Artisanal Fisheries Development Project, Federal Republic of the
Comoros* (1979), the appraisal team found that government officials were unable to provide basic statistics on Gross Domestic Product, balance of payments, and recent agricultural
production or consumption. Lacking baseline data for the project including numbers "employed" in artisanal fishing and
actual fish stocks, the appraisal team could not even estimate
economic rates of return. The same criteria are essentially used
in ADB and ADF appraisal reports; however, in the latter case,
there is some consideration given to "sound developmental"
banking—evidence of the developmental character of the project is required. Some officials have questioned the use of some
of these indicators, arguing that such indicators imply a degree
of technical competence not possible if basic statistical information is unavailable.

If the appraisal report is positive (i.e., the technical, economic, and financial viability standards have been met), then a

"working group" at the interdepartmental level is established. The task of the working group is to refine the appraisal report in preparation for meeting with the loan committee chaired by a vice president. This loan committee examines the policy-relevant questions found in the appraisal report. What political conditions are necessary for the project's success? What specific governmental policies need to be implemented for the project's success? Still, direct criticism of the government's policy is usually "thinly disguised" with secretariat officials "playing it safe." This policy component not explicitly found in the appraisal study has become increasingly important, as shown in chapter 5.

Upon the president's approval of the loan committee's recommendation, the ADB invites the borrower to participate in actual negotiations for the loan. Which governmental officials are sent may be important in determining the terms of the loan and the conditions of execution. The usual practice is for the borrowing governments to send officials from the finance or treasury ministry to negotiate the loans. These officials, rather than those from the executing agency (e.g., Ministry of Agriculture or Ministry of Transportation), are better positioned and more technically qualified to negotiate loan terms. Often, this means that the executing agency may be unfamiliar with the specifications of the loan, so that in the long run execution of the project suffers.

During these loan negotiations, the legal arrangements and requirements of the loan are specified. The document *General Conditions Applicable to Loan and Guarantee Agreements* (ADB, 1983) outlines the formalities: the loan, service and commitment charges; the currencies; the disbursement of loans including conditions precedent to first disbursement, sufficiency of documentation, maintenance of measures; the provisions for cancellation, suspension, or default; liens, taxes, and restrictions; provisions for enforcing loan agreement through arbitration; and loan termination. Although the language of the loan document contains standard legal provisions, specific clauses are intensely negotiated, as explained in chapter 5.

Following agreement on the text of the loan agreement, a

compendium of documents including the appraisal report and the legal text is submitted to the executive board for final approval. As reported in chapter 2, the executive board increasingly intervenes in the process, taking a more activist role to improve the quality of the project and sharpening the provisions of the loan agreement. Hence, in contrast to the executive board of the World Bank, whose approval is almost a formality with management having great flexibility in determining matters of general policy (Ayres, 1983:66), the ADB executive board still plays a critical role in the process. ADB officials, who have negotiated the loan with the borrowers, become an advocate of the loan in front of the board, even though both executive directors and Bank management are supposed to be working toward approving the best projects.

Before the first funds are disbursed, a list of specific conditions must be met. Disbursement delays have resulted from the failure of governmental agencies to submit the necessary documentation; changes in regimes only exacerbate the delay. The Price Waterhouse report (1977) issued a series of administrative recommendations designed to speed disbursement. Included among the recommendations was the need for a procedures manual (described above), standardized working papers and questionnaires for both government's and Bank's use, and the initiation of direct payment to suppliers and contractors. The Bank has generally revised procedures to comply with these recommendations despite government opposition. Many governments prefer to receive the money themselves so that they disburse funds to the executing agency or the private contractors. Funds transferred through these channels augment national income even if redisbursement occurs very rapidly. So governments have fought to retain their intermediary role for political reasons.

An ADB officer then oversees disbursement according to the schedule and preconditions listed in the agreement. Each disbursement official covers eight countries and as many as eighty projects. The loan officer is charged with supervision of the project, as many as fifteen to twenty-five projects simultaneously. He or she is supposed to be visiting each project four times a year. While this work load does not cause bottlenecks at the loan disbursement stage, it results in inadequate supervision of projects. Officers are able to visit the sites and talk with implementing personnel perhaps once a year. Few functional experts are able to accompany project officers, so technical supervision of projects is lax. In some cases, ADB officials may not have direct access to the borrower's accounting systems, making economic supervision incomplete. According to ADB officials, all governments seem to want more ADB supervision. The governments are unaware of or unable to keep abreast of implementation procedures and problems and hence desire the ADB's help in fulfilling this task. Inadequate supervision often results in contractors coming directly to the ADB to try to expedite payments, even though in most cases the cause of the problem may be a government that has not yet provided appropriate documentation to the ADB.

When the project is completed, the Bank and the executing agency submit a project completion report, a checklist confirming that all of the components of the project have been completed. This report is used as the basis for the post-hoc evaluation report discussed in chapter 9.

The procedures and processes described above lead to the implementation of an ADB-funded project. There are numerous steps in the process where political considerations may intervene. Consultation between ADB and member state officials results in projects. Both politically unstable governments and eager ADB officials seek credit for and have a vested interest in project initiation. The priority given a project in the country's pipeline of projects may be disputed between the two groups of negotiators, although in the final analysis, the priority of the member state is honored. The ability of the appraisal team to conduct financial, technical, and economic viability studies depends on the cooperation of the governments, governments that may be embarrassed by the unavailability of some information and sensitive to the dissemination of other information. Each party may have different ideas concerning the relative weight attached to each component of the appraisal study. At a later stage, ADB officials ask policy relevant questions necessary for project implementation. Such questioning of government policy, sometimes veiled criticism of it, results in political controversy. Political considerations, not technical qualifications, may determine which government officials negotiate final loan provisions with the ADB, the effects of which are felt in project execution. Thus project lending involves negotiations between two sets of officials; the negotiations are embedded in the political process at several critical junctures.

Nonproject lending, or program or sector lending, has been advocated as an approach designed to remedy both haphazard coordination of projects at the country level and flagrant intervention by political authorities. Only 10 percent of ADB expenditures may be used for nonproject lending. But contrary to expectations, such lending is not immune to political influence for two reasons. First, the institutional processes for implementating and supervising nonproject lending, including rehabilitation loans, are much less developed. The criteria used to judge technical, economic, and financial viability on nonproject lending (or rehabilitation loans) are largely unspecified. In the absence of institutionalized procedures, political determinations may more easily intervene. Second, nonproject lending often requires greater participation by governmental authorities because a governmental policy or an entire sector may be targeted. Entrenched governmental interests are often well positioned to oppose intervention by external authorities. Both of these factors lead to increased salience of political factors, as discussed in chapter 5. Politics, indeed, may be exacerbated under nonproject lending, just as it intervened in major policy issues explored in chapter 4.

Policy Debates

African Development Bank members, like members in all economic organizations charged with operational tasks, must confront a number of procedural and substantive policy choices that are apt to divide the membership. In this chapter, I address three such issues, with special attention to the various positions held by different constituencies both within and outside of the organization. Even after the policy choices were made on the role of multinational projects, the membership of extraregional states, and changes in lending priorities, residual controversy remains.

The establishment of the ADB was based on the notion that regional projects, those involving at least several African countries, would receive high priority in the Bank's lending portfolio. Support for the regional project approach was given by many state officials, who believed that the uniqueness of the ADB as an institution would be helpful in accelerating regional economic integration. Yet many states opposed this approach. For example, some of the former French colonies—including Mauritania, Mali, Niger, Senegal, and Chad—argued that states having disadvantageous geographic positions should be given preference for project assistance. Liberia, Nigeria, Sierre Leone, Sudan, and Tunisia also expressed their opposition, contending that such projects are too difficult to implement. Despite this opposition, priority was initially given to multicountry projects—projects designed to further African economic integration. These projects, however, never represented a significant proportion of the ADB lending portfolio.

The problems that have plagued these projects may be illustrated, in part, by an examination of ADB's role in the Panafrican Telecommunications Network (ADB, 1984a). The program began in 1962 to provide telecommunication (phone and
telex) circuits between African countries, bypassing the lines
linking the states with the former colonial powers. In 1968 the
ADB became involved; by 1973 the Bank had assumed a major
role in coordinating the financing and implementation of the
project. Although the Bank has provided only 6.3% of the network's funding requirements (Labotse-Francistown; Lusaka-
Tanzania; Conakry, Mali; Conakry-Sierra Leon links), it is the
coordinator of the system. The task is made more difficult by
the fact that credits are made from the various lending agencies
directly to the governments, without passing through ADB
headquarters. Coordinating project execution has proven difficult because the ADB has limited direct leverage with the other
sources of financing. The result is that projects have consistently remained behind schedule. Despite the addition of new
links, the service has deteriorated due to lack of maintenance,
lack of coordination in signal coding, and interruptions due to
irregular electrical supply. In short, the necessary coordination
between governments for multinational projects to be successful has been very difficult to achieve.

Two other projects further illustrate the problems with funding multinational projects. The first, the Accra-Abidjan Highway, a segment of the Transafrican Highway, has stalled. Neither
country accepted the engineering report, preferring instead to
reroute the road through specific towns. The Ivory Coast, to
express their dissatisfaction with the project, changed to French
technical standards from the English ones used in the original
study (ADB/USAID 1980). The second illustrates how the
failure of states to follow up multinational projects decreases
effectiveness. Liberia and Sierra Leone with ADB funding con-
structed the Mano River Bridge in order to increase interstate
traffic. Yet neither country improved the secondary roads leading to the bridge and Sierra Leone imposed tolls on its side of the
bridge. Four years after completion, only ten cars a day cross the

bridge, well below the number estimated to make the project economically remunerative (ADB/USAID 1980).

Given these difficulties in managing and implementing multinational projects, ADB loans for regional projects have dwindled. Between 1974 and 1983 two projects in East Africa were financed under multinational auspices and fifteen projects in West Africa, for a value of $7 million and $130 million respectively. These figures do not include projects located in one country, for example a road that eventually is to become a part of a trans-African network (Transafrican Highway). The problem of arrears (see chapter 5) has made multinational projects even less attractive. According to ADB officials, if one country is in arrears in a multinational project, funds for entire projects are held up. Given this penalty, some of the economically stronger partner states participating in a multinational project have chosen to pay off the neighboring country's arrears. In the mid-1980s the Ivory Coast paid for the arrears of a joint Togolese, Ghanaian, and Ivorian project in order to keep the funds flowing to that project and to other Ivorian projects.

The issue of multinational projects is no longer a politically controversial question within the ADB. Most members have acknowledged the failure of ADB to make a unique contribution in this area. They are more sanguine about the prospects of getting the necessary multinational cooperation for such projects. Members have not, however, given up on such projects. Initially the ADB set an upper limit of eight million units of account on lending for multinational projects, but in 1982, all such ceilings were removed (Gardiner and Pickett, 1984: 73).

Other policy issues have received disproportionate attention. The first, an organizational decision having substantive implications, concerns the admission of extraregionals. Although the issue was actually settled quickly, the decision profoundly altered the procedural and substantive characteristics of the organization. The second, the role of agricultural projects in the Bank's lending portfolio, has been a persistently controversial issue. Each of these policy issues will be discussed in turn, highlighting the various positions debated within the ADB and between the ADB and its constituent members.

During the discussions leading to the establishment of the ADB, there was virtual consensus that the Bank would be composed of African states only. Among those who, like President Gamal Abdel Nasser of Egypt, envisioned an African institution, some were willing to contribute sizeable financing to achieve this institutional autonomy. But this view was not unanimously shared. Burundi, Uganda, Ivory Coast, and Ghana, for example, sensed that membership for countries outside Africa would not only guarantee additional resources, but would also inspire international confidence in the institution. Others anticipated that African hegemons would try to manipulate the organization. But these reservations were set aside as African states opted "to go it alone." Western scholars viewed restricted membership as a weakness. As John White stated, "Indeed, the historical record of the institution is a record of little else but blocked initiatives and unresolved dilemmas. By comparison with the Inter-American bank and even the Asian bank, the African bank appears at first sight to be fatally lacking both in momentum and in the resources by which momentum might be generated" (1972:131).

Fifteen years later as the amount of contributions that African states were able to make to the Bank declined and as the Bank's difficulties with borrowing in the international capital markets became manifest, some members began to accept the principle that the capital stock should be open to extraregional states, subject to the strict proviso that the "African character" of the institution be preserved. Both international and domestic factors led to this change in position. The 1973-74 oil crisis wreaked havoc with the vulnerable economies of many members; the promised Arab oil money for assistance never arrived; and most African currencies were inextricably tied to strong outside currencies, such as the American dollar, French franc, or British pound (Bendo-Soupou, 1985:70-73). Lacking funds to invest in projects, unable to borrow internationally, and in arrears on debts, many African states saw no alternative but to open the Bank to extraregional membership. Hence, during the board of governors' meeting in Libreville in 1979, Resolution 02-79 stipulated that the president initiate consultations with extraregionals, study the implications of the change, and submit a report on the matter (ADB, 1978).

The decision was controversial. Nigeria, Libya, and Algeria were among the most vocal opponents. Each of the states already exerted considerable influence in the ADB by virtue of size and economic prowess; they were apprehensive about having to relinquish any leadership role. Both Libya and Algeria expressed opposition also on ideological grounds—that the regionals were leaving themselves open to unwarranted external influence—in the words of one, expressing "une politique d'abandon." For these countries, ties with external actors should not be renewed. For Algeria, extraregional membership posed a blatant contradiction because extensive efforts had been made to ensure that every institution in Algeria was 100% Algerian. Although Algeria announced it would agree if the majority decided to admit non-Africans, Algeria did disrupt the proceedings with its objections (Fordwor, 1981:105).

Despite this persistent vocal opposition, the board of governors instructed President Fordwor to conduct the necessary negotiations with extraregionals. Fordwor, supportive of extraregional admission, quickly sent out letters communicating the Libreville decision to participants in the African Development Fund, including the non-member states of the Soviet Union, People's Republic of China, Austria, United Arab Emirates, and Qatar. He then arranged a series of visits to seven countries, including Canada, the United States, the Federal Republic of Germany, the United Kingdom, Japan, France, and Denmark (where he met with the whole Nordic group). The results of this series of bilateral discussions were favorable: all governments consulted accepted the principle of membership. Some questions were raised, however: What was going to be the ratio between convertible and nonconvertible currency? Could the ADB handle administratively the substantial augmentation of financial resources projected by the admission of extraregionals? Did Africa really have the absorptive capacity to use the added infusion of resources? Under certain circumstances, might not special majorities be required? And all concurred that representation by only three extraregional states on the twelve-member executive board was inadequate (ADB, 1979a; ADB, 1979b).

Several countries expressed reasons why participation might be problematic. France, in particular, feared that membership would interfere with traditional spheres of French economic and political influence. The Belgians, Dutch, and Italians had serious doubts that such an institution could succeed, but were nevertheless supportive. The United States saw the admission as a way to wean the Africans from the British and French. For the African members, extraregional membership was a potential avenue to the international capital markets and to increased institutional visibility in Africa itself. As one African government official lamented, "Pendant mon passage au ministère des finances de mon pays, je n'ai jamais été mis au courant de l'existence de la B.A.D. [ADB]" (Bendo-Soupou, 1985:70).

There was sufficient consensus among the extraregionals to begin multilateral negotiations; Horst Moltrecht of the Federal Republic of Germany was elected coordinator of the group. Conferences were held in Rabat (27-29 November 1978), Abidjan (11-12 January 1979), and London (13-14 February 1979). The consultations resulted in the following compromises:

A. The extraregionals agreed to $6.3 billion annual lending as advocated by the regionals, even though the extraregionals were skeptical about the ADB's capacity to administer that amount.

B. Both regionals and extraregionals agreed that with the augmentation of new capital, loans could be increased from a maximum of $6 million to $25 million per project. The extraregionals advocated caution in removing this ceiling altogether, fearing that the countries might not have the capacity to absorb such funds.

C. No quick compromise was reached concerning the composition of paid-in contributions. The regionals argued that they should be able to make their paid-up contribution in local currency. The extraregionals contended that one-half of the contributions should be in hard currency and one-half in local currency. The extraregionals eventually agreed to accept 25% paid in local currency for the regional members.

D. The extraregionals agreed to keep the ADB and ADF as completely separate institutions. The regionals concurred, but stipulated that admission to the ADB should not result in decreased funding for the concessional African Development Fund. Indeed, many regionals felt that appropriate contributions to the Fund should be a prerequisite for participation quotas in the Bank.

E. Extraregionals agreed to a 2:1 regional to extraregional ratio in the ADB structure. To accommodate this ratio, the number of executive directors was enlarged to eighteen members to permit participation by the smaller extraregional members. Without enlargement, extraregionals would not have joined. This two-thirds to one-third ratio would also be preserved in voting: each state would receive 625 membership votes, with the number of votes apportioned according to the shares of the capital stock held by that member.

F. Extraregionals supported the proposition that countries not joining the ADB would be ineligible to compete for procurement. However, the same group proposed that the ADB accept the Organization for Economic Cooperation and Development's (OECD) Development Assistance Committee guidelines, which allow less-developed countries outside of Africa to participate in procurement. This provision was ultimately rejected by the regional members.

G. Extraregionals wanted the Bank to consider recruiting and appointing new professional staff from extraregional states. Although the extraregionals received no guarantee that this would actually happen, Bank management agreed to consider the option.

H. Finally, extraregionals were fundamentally in agreement that the "African character" of the Bank should be preserved, meaning that the president would always be an African (elected by majority, including a majority of regional members), that loans would be confined to Africa, and that the headquarters of the organization would always be located on the continent.

These compromises essentially reflected a pragmatic approach. Because "the African character" of the Bank could not be adequately defined, rules were devised to ensure that African members would retain control. Once devised, the negotiations were conducted very rapidly, because the extraregionals were all members of the African Development Fund and, hence, basically familiar with the operations of the Bank. Many of these same countries already had discussed comparable issues in applying for admission to the Inter-American Development Bank (IDB).

The Bank's responses to the points raised by the extraregional group were given equally as rapidly. They agreed to the 12:6 ratio of the executive directors, conceding that this ratio did not jeopardize the African character of the Bank. And they acquiesced to the demand that the regionals pay some contributions in convertible currency. But Bank management proposed that regional countries be given credit for payments already made in convertible currency, effectively easing the payment burden for regional members. Pending satisfactory resolution of this problem, Bank management recommended that the board of governors approve a resolution supporting extraregional membership and approving the necessary amendments to the charter.

Thus, beginning in 1982 the extraregionals assumed their new position in the Bank as full members. Then Vice President Babacar N'Diaye (*Afrique*, 1983:45) stated "C'est un mariage mixte. Ce qui compte maintenant, c'est que les enfants soient beaux." Some sporadic opposition to their membership persists. As one official summarizes, when extraregionals push in a certain policy direction against the regional consensus, the Algerians, Libyans, or Nigerians tend to reiterate with "we told you so." But the *issue* of extraregional admission has been largely resolved, and the substantial augmentation of financial resources and project lending has tended to mute the criticism.

What impact has the admission of the extraregionals had on the Bank as an institution? On the amount and direction of Bank lending? On economic development policy followed? Immediate financial resources were augmented by extraregional

Table 4. African Development Bank Group, Disbursement by
Sector, 1974-86 (%)

Sector	1974	1975	1976	1977	1978	1979	1980	1981	1982	1983	1984	1985	1986
Agriculture	17	17	14	15	16	20	17	26	23	22	23	19	20
Transport	56	40	39	29	31	29	38	27	27	28	27	29	26
Telecommun- ications	3	5	4	9	4	5	2	2	2	3	4	5	5
Water supply and sewage	3	8	10	11	19	15	12	11	11	8	9	10	9
Power supply	8	18	13	18	14	14	12	12	10	9	10	10	10
Industry	—	1	6	8	6	5	7	8	11	9	6	8	9
Development banks	13	13	14	9	10	8	6	9	10	10	7	10	14
Education	—	—	—	1	4	2	4	2	6	5	8	6	6
Health	—	—	—	1	1	1	2	2	1	6	5	2	3

Note: Percentages may not total 100% due to rounding errors. Source:
African Development Bank Planning and Research Department. *Compendium of Statistics* (1984, 1987).

contributions as shown in table 4. Although ADB officials had
begun to win the confidence of the investment community
before extraregional membership, in 1982 the Bank retained the
services of Kidder, Peabody and Co. to act as financial advisor.
S. Melvin Rines of Kidder, Peabody and Co. describes the process
by which the ADB was rated, "The rating process took almost a
year. It was by all measures the lengthiest and most thorough
rating process that most of us who do this had ever seen. This
was the first multilateral development bank in fifteen years to
receive an initial rating. The world had changed. The rating
procedures had changed. There was more skepticism out there
on the part of analysts. They wanted to bore in deeply on the
loan portfolio, looking at specific examples of loans—the good,
the bad, the indifferent" (quoted in Parker, 1986:8). In January
1984, Moody's Investors Service and Fitch Investors Service gave
the ADB a top triple-A rating and Standard and Poors gave the
Bank a double-A rating. These excellent ratings were achieved
in part because the extraregionals had given economic support
and political legitimacy to the organization. With extraregional

members, the ADB is able to borrow successfully on the international credit/bond market.

In many respects, the extraregionals have not substantially altered the processes employed at the African Development Bank. At the level of the executive directors, getting a loan through the pipeline has slowed with the more careful scrutinizing of loans. Loans are no longer granted automatically, even though more funds are available. The ADB process has been lengthened with the initiation of post hoc evaluations conducted at the insistence of the extraregionals. But much to the amazement of some of the officials in the ADB secretariat, political jockeying within the secretariat remains about the same. The extraregionals have acted just like the regionals in the personnel process, actively lobbying for nationals to receive key positions, even when some of these people may not be the most qualified for the position. In the words of one secretariat official, "we thought the non-regionals [extraregionals] wouldn't do things like that—they are worse than the Africans."

What has changed is that the extraregionals have been trying to push new policy orientations. A number of these new orientation will be discussed in more detail in chapter 5, but briefly, the extraregionals have added the following provisions: (1) Loan agreements need to include more specific pre-loan conditions, so that borrowing governments and agencies are able to utilize funds once they become available; (2) Loan agreements should include specific provisions for financial accountability, including use of standardized methods and provisions for repayment; (3) Attached to the loans, either in a formal or informal manner, should be some kinds of conditionality—specific advice that the government should follow in order to ensure better use of the funds; (4) Failure to repay loans according to the agreed timetable should result in sanctioning of members; (5) The private sector should be increasingly involved in the ownership and management of projects; and (6) Countries need to consider non-project loans, including loans for rehabilitation of existing projects.

As a result of the extraregionals bringing these issues to the organizational agenda, there has been, as reported in chapter 2, increased controversy in the executive board. Although there is disagreement between the extraregionals and regionals on the specific implementation of these agenda items, persistent cleavages in the board of directors have not materialized.

The admission of the extraregionals is an organizational issue that will continue to have profound repercussions on substantive policy. One issue in which differences between the approach of regional and extraregional members is evident is agricultural policy. The critical issue of agriculture examined in the next section remains a major source of controversy both within the organization and between the organization and its cofinancing partners, as discussed in chapter 7.

Among all the development institutions and governments operating bilateral projects in Africa, there is widespread consensus that deterioration of the agricultural sector is the key problem on the continent. According to Gardiner and Pickett (1984:120) and widely substantiated during the 1970s, per capita agricultural output declined at an average annual rate of 1.4%. Specifically, food production per capita declined at an average annual rate of 1.2%. Although there is no disagreement about the statistics, there is disagreement about both the cause of these declines and the proper strategies needed to alleviate the problem.

A comparison of the approaches followed by the World Bank and the ADB with respect to agriculture permits us to examine the differences. In the World Bank's *Accelerated Development in Sub-Saharan Africa: An Agenda for Action* (1981a), agricultural deterioration is attributed to domestic trade and exchange rate policies; pricing, taxing, and exchange rate policies have been consistently biased against agriculture. Given this diagnosis of the problem, the preferred policies include correcting overvalued exchange rates, improving price incentives for exports and for domestic agriculture, and reducing direct government control in the sector. According to this analysis, if these market-type measures are implemented by the state, then the agricultural sector will improve. The 1984 World Bank document

Toward Sustained Development modified the *Accelerated Development* position slightly, making particular note of the role of the external environment in causing agricultural decline. The views of the World Bank are widely shared by members of the donor community, including most extraregional members of the ADB.

In contrast, although the African Development Bank itself has not published a document elucidating a theory of economic development, Bank officials suggest that they are taking "guidance" from the Organization of African Unity's *Lagos Plan of Action* (1980). Specifically, the Lagos Plan stresses African self-sufficiency in several broad areas. The first priority is achieving self-sufficient agricultural production. To increase food production, emphasis is placed on increasing the volume of resources to agriculture, encouraging small farmers and agricultural cooperatives to achieve higher levels of productivity, and stimulating cultivation of native cereals (millet, maize, and sorghum) over more expensive imports. Peasant farming is championed over grandiose projects. As an aid to achieving national self-sufficiency, intra-African trade must be enhanced, leading to an African common market by the year 2000. Although the ADB has been loathe to accept a doctrinaire approach, regional members insist that food self-sufficiency is of critical importance. Increased intra-African trade leading to the establishment of an African common market is the preferred method to foster these goals.

All of these documents are woefully inadequate guides to making policy for the agricultural sector. The eight-page treatment given agriculture in the Lagos Plan is superficial. As John Ravenhill describes it, the document is "prone to tautologies and largely meaningless exhortations" (1986b:90). Absent from the plan are detailed policy proposals and any realistic evaluation of potential costs. Agricultural self-sufficiency, in fact, may be very costly, both economically and politically. Similarly, the *Accelerated Development* section on agriculture displays undue optimism regarding prospects for traditional agricultural exports (Ravenhill, 1986a:15-17). The report fails to acknowledge "the fallacy of composition" problem, that with relatively inelastic demand for tropical export crops, production increases are apt to lead to sagging prices (Ravenhill, 1986a:17). Perhaps most important, the *Accelerated Development* plan does not set priorities or show any historical perspective (Green and Allison, 1986:73). Even the *Toward Sustained Development* document does not give detailed consideration to or even discuss the policy implications of specializing in traditional agricultural exports (Ravenhill, 1986a:5).

As inadequate as these documents may be, they have stimulated both governments and the international lending institutions to give added attention to agriculture. Within the ADB, the "return" to agriculture was controversial, as seen at the board of governors' meeting in 1982 (Lusaka) and in the 1983 (Nairobi) meeting. The extraregionals, especially the Netherlands and Italy, voiced support for reestablishing priority to the agriculture sector. Regional members were ambivalent. Drawing on the Lagos Plan, which still viewed industrialization as a panacea, Libya insisted that there be no decrease in lending for industrial development. Other members, both regional and extraregional, argued that agriculture and industrialization were complementary; agricultural development was a necessary pre condition for industrialization to take place (Please and Amoako, 1986:138). Hence, while priority needs to be given to agriculture at the outset, this is not a substitute for industrialization.

A close examination of table 4 suggests that the agricultural sector has received an increasing percentage of ADB spending, ranging from 17% in 1975 to 26% in 1981, down to 23% in 1984 and 20% in 1986. Between 1967 and 1973, the agricultural sector received almost 16% of ADB group annual lending. The recent decrease in loans to agriculture can be explained, in part, by the keen competition among development agencies for viable agricultural projects (see chapters 7 and 8).

The ADB's commitment to agriculture also reflects governmental priorities. Some states have been particularly predisposed toward submitting and receiving aid to the agricultural sector. Gardiner and Pickett (1984:128) found that in the period 1967-81, of the forty-seven countries borrowing, seventeen allocated more than 30% of their total borrowing to agriculture,

Table 5. Distribution of ADB and ADF Agricultural Lending by
Subsector, 1977-82 (%)

Sub-Sectors	1977			1978			1979		
	ADB	ADF	Total	ADB	ADF	Total	ADB	ADF	Total
Agro-industry	76.1	22.2	39.0	46.7	13.2	14.3	56.9	—	26.5
Food crops and rural development	23.9	77.8	61.0	12.8	52.5	33.2	38.3	79.5	60.4
Cash crops	—	—	—	29.7	13.2	43.7	4.7	5.2	4.9
Livestock	—	—	—	—	15.5	4.7	—	9.6	5.1
Fisheries	—	—	—	—	—	—	—	5.7	3.1
Forestry	—	—	—	10.8	—	2.4	—	—	—
Lines of credit	—	—	—	—	5.6	1.7	—	—	—

while ten countries used between 20% and 30% of their funds
for agriculture, and twenty countries used less than 20% of their
funds borrowed for agricultural purposes. Yet among the governments committing this lower percentage were many that had
the most severe food problems.

Relatively modest amounts of funding committed to agriculture also reflect the realization that these projects are among
the most difficult to implement, particularly as they encompass
broadly "rural development." These projects involve a plethora
of different governmental agencies, whose work must be closely
coordinated; they require the transfer of capital (both physical
and monetary) to remote areas. Successful completion depends,
in part, on other largely uncontrollable factors, weather, and
pest cycles. Hence planners desiring a high probability of success do not always select agricultural projects.

How the funding is allocated in the agricultural sector is of
particular salience. Outside critics of the ADB argue that money
is really not going to produce self-sufficient agriculture as proposed by the Lagos Plan of Action, but rather supports agri-
business. The statistics reported in table 5 do not substantiate
this criticism. If lending within the agricultural sector is disag-
gregated, the share of loans destined to agro-industry has declined from 39% in 1977 to nearly 9% in 1982, whereas the
funds allocated to food crops and rural development have in-

Table 5. (continued)

	1980			1981			1982		
Sub-Sectors	ADB	ADF	Total	ADB	ADF	Total	ADB	ADF	Total
Agro-industry	—	9.9	8.0	22.7	7.9	12.6	13.8	3.9	8.8
Food crops and rural development	35.6	68.5	62.5	59.0	58.0	58.4	66.6	75.4	71.1
Cash crops	—	14.7	12.0	—	7.9	5.3	9.8	—	4.8
Livestock	64.4	—	11.8	18.3	—	5.7	—	3.5	1.7
Fisheries	—	—	—	—	—	—	—	—	—
Forestry	—	—	—	—	7.7	5.3	—	10.3	5.3
Lines of credit	—	6.9	5.7	—	18.5	12.7	9.8	6.9	8.3

Source: African Development Bank Planning and Research Department. *Compendium of Statistics* (1984, 1987).

creased from 61% to over 71% during the same time interval. And the funds allocated to cash crops have vacillated with a downward trend—from 43.7% to 4.9% to 12% to 4.8%. The long maturation time involved in funding cash crop projects may be the explanation for the substantial change in funding levels. Nevertheless, the data supports the argument that within the agriculture sector, ADB's reorientation has been toward projects enhancing domestic food self-sufficiency.

The renewed emphasis on agriculture can also be attributed to the increase of concessional funding through the African Development Fund. The position of the extraregionals supporting agricultural sector over other sectors has been well articulated in the ADF.

Not only has the ADB given priority to agriculture in terms of loan allocations, and to the support of food crops more specifically, the ADB research unit has examined in detail a number of sector-specific problems. In one research paper, the Planning and Research Department has suggested approaches to eliminate several bottlenecks in the food distribution cycle. For example, support might be given to improving packaging (and hence food preservation), to funding applied research centers, or to aiding in information dissemination through the existing yet moribund farm extension services. More attention might be focused on funding feeder trunk roads in rural areas to facilitate the movement of food stuffs to local and/or regional markets (ADB Planning and Research Department, 1983).

Similarly, Bank researchers have concluded that small-scale enterprises for local food processing need to be supported. Such enterprises would be geographically closer to the source of food and less dependent on infrastructure, institutions, and trained work force for successful handling. Researchers have also reiterated the need for freer pricing, arguing that African farmers will respond to price incentives by increasing production. However, the pricing issue has been and continues to be a particularly controversial one. The consensus among ADB economists seems to be that in some member states agricultural prices must be changed, but that price decontrols alone will not solve the economic problems of the rural sector. They forecast that price gains to producers may actually be nominal because of domestic inflation. In some countries, changing agricultural prices may be politically impossible if the governing regime wants to remain in power.

As shown in table 4, other sectors do continue to receive substantial ADB group support. The share to transport has declined from 56% in 1974 to 26% in 1986, but that percentage is still high. The combined percentage of funding going to industry and development banks supporting industry has increased, reaching 23% in 1986. These funds were being used to support new enterprises in key service industries, direct rehabilitation loans and indirect loans through national development banks, and loans for private sector promotion (although no more than 10% of loans may be made without governmental guarantees). In much of the discussion among Bank officials and governments, support for the other sectors is justified on the basis of each sector's contribution to agricultural development.

Among the three issues examined, the decision accepting extra-regional membership was resolved most rapidly with the most significant outcome for the organization. Although persistent cleavages in the governing structures of the organization do not exist, there are differences in policy orientations that remain salient, including the agricultural policy discussed above. There are also differences held generally by regional and extraregional members on two questions relating to the ADB's interactions with borrowing governments: Should the ADB try to influence borrowing government's policies? If so, what techniques of influence does the ADB have toward borrowing governments? These questions are addressed in chapter 5.

The ADB's Influence on Borrowing States

International economic organizations whose tasks are limited to service activities such as providing information to states and performing studies commissioned by and acceptable to states are less likely to evoke political controversy than are organizations whose tasks are rule creating or operational. Multilateral development banks like the African Development Bank are charged with initiating and managing projects. For many projects to be successful, governmental policies must be changed. In other words, development finance institutions must be able to affect state policies if they are to be successful in achieving specific project goals and if they are to achieve more comprehensive development goals.

Traditionally, scholars examining the origins of national governmental policy have focused on internal determinants of policy, including such factors as individual leadership, governmental structures, and societal processes (Rosenau, 1966). Often excluded from consideration were external influences, including international organizations, although studies by B.E. Matecki (1957), Ronald Meltzer (1976), and Margaret Karns and Karen Mingst (1987) are the exceptions. The "dependencia" writers have provided the most convincing empirical evidence for impacts of international organizations on state domestic policy. Bettin Hürni (1980) and Cheryl Payer (1974, 1982), among others, assert that both the World Bank and the IMF are postwar economic institutions established to conform to a liberal view of world order, institutionalized under American economic hegemony, having direct policy effects on their Third World constituency. These international organizations are viewed as advocating and imposing directly on national decision makers policies inimical to their national economic interests.

In an era when most IGOs are dismissed as "benign," how can the multilateral development banks affect national policy? What techniques of influence do they have at their disposal? How potent are these techniques? As David Baldwin argues, "neither policy analysts nor power analysts have given much attention to the instruments or techniques of influence" (1985:9). An examination of such techniques is critical to support of the argument that economic organizations are highly political institutions.

At its origin, the ADB had such limited economic resources and low public visibility that few countries applied for project loans. Those that applied usually received funding with few preconditions attached. Neither the few professionals in the ADB nor national bureaucracies in member states were able to evaluate the projects or to supervise closely their implementation. The same officials were unlikely to consider trying to intervene in a borrowing state's macroeconomic policies. They certainly had insufficient visibility to have fundamentally altered the economic thinking of national officials. However, in the 1970s with the expanded professional capability of the ADB staff, and in the early 1980s with the adhesion of the extraregionals, the executive directors began to consider more carefully the range of techniques available to them to try to influence state policy. It was recognized that influencing the direction of state policy was a necessary prerequisite for project success. The four techniques that the ADB has utilized are discussed in turn below. Use of the techniques tends to make the Bank/borrowing state relationship a solidly political, oftimes controversial, one.

One technique of influence that IGOs have utilizes the organization's knowledge and expertise. That expertise can be harnessed to convince states to examine problems in a different way or to try new policy directions. The World Bank has often been in the forefront of thinking about economic development. For example, following President Robert McNamara's speech on 24 September 1973, the World Bank committed itself to a basic human needs approach. As Robert Ayres (1983) describes, the World Bank has played an important role in the international marketplace of ideas, largely as a consciousness raiser about development.

During the first two decades, the ADB was insufficiently strong economically and politically to be a stimulator of ideas. There is evidence from the 1980s, however, that ADB officials have become effective communicators of ideas from other development institutions to African states and have adopted and assimilated the ideas as their own. As President N'Diaye stated in 1989, "We have realized that project financing alone won't lead to development. We need to integrate *ideas* which will help shape the development of the continent. Ideas are more important than resources. Our dream is to transform the bank into a center of knowledge for African development. We must serve as a catalyst" (quoted in Thurow, 1989:1).

Two examples of the ADB's stimulation of development ideas merit discussion. In April 1986, the ADB convened a seminar to study the links between ecological deterioration and economic decline in Africa. The Bank saw this project as a long-term commitment "aimed at sensitizing African and international opinion to the grave danger of ecological deterioration, assisting regional member countries to evolve environmentally based development strategies, and drawing implications for ADB's own operational policies" (U.S. House of Representatives, 1986). The Bank has not heretofore been at the forefront of examining environmental-economic linkages, but taking the lead from such institutions as the World Bank, the ADB is involved in trying to educate member states about the potential linkages and therefore influence state policy through the realm of ideas.

A second example may be found in the efforts of President N'Diaye to reorganize the Bank to enhance its role as a private sector promoter, by helping identify private-sector investment opportunities for Africa entrepreneurs (U.S. House of Representatives, 1986). The ADB was not the originator of the private enterprise approach to economic development, nor are many Bank officials confirmed advocates of the approach. But the ADB has been reorganized to consider private enterprise contributions; it has revised its industrial-sector policy paper to facilitate lending to the private sector without government guarantees and has made it easier for the Bank to take equity positions in African enterprises. These are the same enterprises that kept many countries economically viable with their informal market trading. By its promotion of the private sector, the ADB as an institution is influencing state members, adding African legitimacy to ideas usually identified with Western economic specialists.

A second important technique that multilateral development banks use to influence state borrowers is to negotiate preconditions that states must accept prior to first disbursement. A group of standard clauses accompany most loans. The borrowing governments usually agree to the following: (1) to submit a budget showing their share of the cost of the project; (2) to meet any cost overruns; (3) to provide evidence that complementary/cofinancing funds have been secured; (4) to ensure that no local taxes or customs are financed out of proceeds; and (5) to submit proof that it is on-lending the loans to a specific agency with no more restrictive conditions than those imposed by the ADB itself.

As the ADB has developed as an institution, it has increasingly added more preconditions relating to management conditions obligatory before disbursement. For example, borrowing governments must set up a "project unit" to manage the project and agree to hold periodic meetings; they must agree to recruit certain types of specialists, available during critical junctures of the project; they must guarantee that ADB officials approve consultant contracts and subproject appraisal reports; and finally, the governments must guarantee that the facilities built be run properly. The latter is a broad precondition just beginning to be included.

Preconditions specifying the financial arrangements of a project tend to be the most numerous. Recipient governments have to provide evidence for continued financing of recurrent costs, maintenance, and inventory of equipment, as well as provisions for a managing agency having working capital equivalent to several months' operations. Gradually these provisions have become more detailed as ADB has sought tighter controls. In the Soubre hydroelectric project, the Ivory Coast had to present not only an elaborate schedule of repayments, but also report procedures designed to ensure that bills presented by the contractors were honored. Increasingly, ADB seeks guarantees that governments have adequate provisions for continued financial viability of a project by including clauses forbidding additional capital expenditures without express Bank approval (Madagascar-Panganale Canal Development), subordinating other loans to the indebtedness of the borrower (Zambia—rehabilitation of copper-mining industry), and forbidding governments to exempt the project unit from payments of residual surplus to the treasury department and obligations of payment of capital charges (Ethiopia—financing of telecommunications). Also ubiquitous are provisions that require governments to permit a project unit to alter the scale of charges to keep the operation on a sound financial basis or that require the governments to review pricing policies, so that farmer incentives are guaranteed (Egypt— agricultural development project). In only two cases has the ADB required that the governments agree not to permit the construction of parallel or competing infrastructure before the pending funded project is saturated (Madagascar-Panganale Canal Development and the Comoros artisanal fisheries project). This analysis of the financial preconditions of the loans indicates that provisions have become progressively more numerous and more technically complex. Borrowing governments are obligated to show that the project will be profitable by assuring ADB officials that pricing for services be based on market criteria and by restricting competition.

In only isolated examples has the ADB attached loan preconditions linked to broader development issues. In one case, the government had to provide evidence that the project was part of a more comprehensive plan (Tunisia—water supply); in another, the government promised to improve connecting services to ensure viability of a project (Tunisia—Mahdia rural development), while in another, all the governments participating in a multinational project had to standardize regulations to facilitate free movement of people and goods. How governments show to ADB's satisfaction that these conditions have been fulfilled has been ambiguous in most cases. The use of preconditions illustrates that ADB officials want governments to place projects in a more comprehensive economic development framework. Whether or not loan preconditions are the proper instrument to force discussion of such issues is debatable.

The imposition of more preconditions, more substantive provisions, and more general provisions has been an important instrument utilized by the ADB to try to direct governments to implement and manage more economically viable projects. Use of preconditions does often result in disbursement delays; governments need more time to comply and the ADB requires additional time to evaluate implementing measures. If the preconditions are not accepted by the borrowing country, the usual procedure is to announce that negotiations have not yet been finished, pending the renegotiation of the preconditions.

These preconditions are often discussed by policy makers. Should conditions be accepted when they take management decisions out of the hands of national personnel? Is approval by an external actor such as ADB management a derogation of national sovereignty? Should a funding agency be allowed to dictate the future course of the project—whether expansion or competition be allowed? Particularly controversial, should the ADB be allowed to suggest prices of a commodity produced from the project (agricultural prices or user fees for infrastructure) as part of preconditions? Should the national governments accept preconditions that tie them to certain strategies of economic development? Although ADB members question the content of specific pre-loan conditions, most accept the preconditions. The funds are needed; without them, there would be no project. The preconditions are the outcome of a lengthy process of negotiations between borrowers and lenders. As the preconditions move beyond the technical financial provisions to the policy conditions listed above, controversy between Bank officials and recipient countries increases.

The ADB has traditionally shied away from imposing explicit conditionality as identified with the International Monetary Fund and to a lesser extent the World Bank. In the words of one official, the ADB is afraid of being "IMFized." The ADB has, nevertheless, begun to move in this direction, albeit timidly and implicitly. In most cases, ADB officials *suggest* that if the government does not undertake measures *leading* in a certain direction (often toward the *eventual* use of the market pricing system), then the country is warned that they will have difficulty in obtaining future loans from the ADB. This policy dialogue is a politically preferable approach, purportedly involving less direct interference in a government's internal affairs. It recognizes that national decision makers retain the ability to undertake independent action.

This noncoercive approach has met with some success. For example, in the words of ADB officials, they "induced" Liberia to establish a pricing committee to determine farm-gate prices of palm oil as a way to protect small-scale oil palm cultivators. The ADB "insisted" and "succeeded" in making Tanzania raise tariffs for infrastructure services, despite the prevailing governmental view that such services represented a public service. And the ADB "induced" Kenya into accepting more decentralized structures of administration through the creation of financially independent township districts in the Nyeri-Nanyki Water Sewage project (ADB Group, 1981).

The executive directors (specifically the executive director representing the country) most often communicate positions of a policy dialogue to national authorities during periodic country visits usually early in project negotiations. Some specific conditions are not explicitly recorded in the loan agreement or included in the pre-loan conditions.

Follow-up investigations to measure relative compliance with ADB directives or suggestions are lax. This weakness can be explained by the fundamental disagreement found within the ADB itself over the appropriateness of this ADB role and a contentious debate over the motivating philosophies underlying conditionality measures. Conditionality implies the rewarding of those who undertake specified reforms. Loans are given when specific policy guidelines are followed. Views vary about the propriety of such measures. Some ADB members support strict IMF conditionalities, others oppose the whole notion, and still others support more flexible and more protracted "IMF-type" guidelines. Lacking a consensus, it is not surprising that the ADB approach to conditionality, attached to specific projects, has been weak with spotty implementation.

The ADB orientation may be changing ("Change at the ADB," 1985:979-85). President N'Diaye in his inaugural address in September 1985 (N'Diaye, 1985) indicated that the thrust of ADB should be toward non-project lending—in other words, more program lending, sectoral loans, and policy advice. As one interviewee aptly observed, as the ADB augments non-project lending, the choices made by the executive directors become more value laden. At the present time, sectoral loans are limited to only 5% of all loans. To obtain these highly competitive sectoral loans, priority is given to countries under IMF agreements as monitored by the World Bank. This "temporary" institutional limitation is self-imposed, as officials have acknowledged that they do not possess sufficient expertise to appraise sectoral lending. In 1985 ADB began to issue country-level macroeconomic studies as a basis for determining the Bank's sectoral lending and country programming. The Ethiopian report (ADB, 1985b) was among the first. This report tread a precarious balance between criticism of the regime for failure of its agricultural policy and "faint" praise for social progress. The study is to be a basis for agricultural sectoral lending to Ethiopia.

When the ADB does decide to offer policy advice, it is guided principally by the Lagos Plan of Action (OAU, 1980). Supported by the ideologically legitimate Organization of African Unity, in contrast to the "tainted" IMF, ADB advice may be more acceptable. But neither the ideological legitimacy of the Lagos Plan nor the competency of the policy advice derived from the Lagos

Plan may be the best explanation for ADB's derived legitimacy in giving policy advice. Since the early 1980s, member countries have experienced such overwhelming economic difficulties, that increasingly they will attempt any policy suggested, even those seemingly at variance with their overall economic development plans. As one interviewee described, some countries just submit lists of things needed to help them alleviate balance of payment difficulties; the ADB staff then struggles to devise a coherent fundable package, often including policy advice and conditions. As the economic conditions in member countries continue to deteriorate, advice is more readily heeded.

Generally, those officials both within and outside ADB agree that the ADB has not put enough pressure on countries to change policies that inhibit the viability of projects, sectors, or programs. In some countries the ADB has fewer viable techniques at its disposal. But the fact that the World Bank through IMF involvement has been advocating conditionality has stimulated ADB's adoption.

The World Bank's goal of seeking ADB involvement in imposing conditionality has been made explicit, "we would expect AFDB [ADB] to support, through its resources and dialogue, the World Bank in its role of stimulating policy reforms in Africa" (World Bank, 1985). World Bank officials contend that the ADB, as a regional organization enjoying a high degree of legitimacy in Africa, can be a useful "go-between" with African governments, muting criticisms of policy reforms, even "cushioning conditionalities." But World Bank officials have stated that they "understand that there may be disincentives" to ADB's involvement in all aspects of conditionality (World Bank, 1985). The challenge, as recognized by ADB officials, is to maintain the ADB's legitimacy, as it simultaneously supports subtle conditionalities. While there is consensus not to link the ADB too closely with these other institutions, there is also growing belief that some conditionality, albeit less rigidly free market and less tied to an absolute time table, may be the appropriate way to proceed—even if such actions create controversy between the Bank managers and recipient governments.

Another technique that the ADB has begun to utilize within the last few years is sanctions imposed for payment arrears. In contrast to positive policy advice, sanctions are a negative instrument having far-reaching consequences. Sanctions for arrears punish borrowers by suspending project disbursements and under most extreme cases by stopping disbursement for all projects and suspending consideration of all projects in the pipeline.

Arrears on loan repayments became a discernible problem after 1981, in part because loans for projects funded in the 1970s began to fall due at a time when national economies were deteriorating. Concern for arrears and attempts to remedy the situation became a critical issue for the extraregional donors as well as for the international capital markets, which had begun to judge the ADB in terms of the timeliness of loan repayments in preparation for the Bank's rating review.

As a result, the board of directors in 1982 began to apply sanctions to countries in arrears at least six months. The sanctions were to be applied selectively—stipulating a series of measures that Bank management could do, including the possibility that no sanctions would be applied if arrears were due to a currency exchange difference or if the amount of arrears was insignificant compared to the total amount billed. This flexible policy proved not to elicit much response from delinquent clients. Hence, beginning 1 January 1985, disbursements on loans to governments in arrears six months were suspended. The six-month provision is relatively lenient, compared to the World Bank policy that begins cutting new funds to states seventy-five days in arrears. Three months later, if still in arrears, the ADB suspends disbursements for all loans granted to the borrower, including consideration of new loans. The sanctions are cross-effective; arrears in the ADB evoke sanctions from the ADF and vice versa (ADB, 1984b, 1985a).

The arrears policy was hotly contested within the executive board. While all members agreed that some type of penalties for arrears must be imposed, the stiffness of the provisions, the automaticity by which they are invoked, and the cross-effective

Table 6. Effectiveness of Sanctions for Arrears,
         Sample Period: 31 August 31-October 1985

	African Development Bank (# of countries)	African Development Fund (# of countries)	Nigerian Trust Fund (# of countries)
No change with sanctions	16	16	11
Pay back some	6	1	1
Pay back most	8	4	3
Paid up all/Cleared arrears	7	9	6
Countries under 3d sanction, no loans	17	12	8

Note: Data does not include arrears on multinational projects.
Source: Data compiled by the author from raw data provided by the
African Development Bank group.

linkage between the ADB and ADF were controversial provisions.

Table 6 presents the data on the relative effectiveness of the most stringent sanctioning measures for arrears. In each of the three funds, most countries did not attempt to pay even under sanctions, 43% of countries in the ADB and 53% in the ADF. Some countries cleared all their arrears—19% in the ADB to 30% in the ADF. In each fund, record numbers of countries were under third sanction. This data does not prove that the states actually reacted either to the threat or imposition of sanctions. A country may have decided to repay irrespective of sanctioning. However, the increasingly strict policy toward arrears initiated by the executive directors does indicate renewed willingness of ADB officials to persuade, threaten, and then punish offenders for their transgression of failure to pay. As Baldwin cogently argues, "To make the target of an influence attempt pay a price for noncompliance is to be partially successful. Thus the relevant question is not merely whether compliance was forthcoming, but also whether costs for non-compliance were imposed" (1985:372). Using this logic, the ADB has been successful with the new sanction policy.

The policy has created new dilemmas. If nonpayment of arrears persists, then that country's subscription shares are made available to other members. By the end of 1985, a total of 7,912 shares had been transferred from sixteen regional members to other regional members: Botswana (2,616 shares), Ethiopia (1,000 shares), Egypt (4,056 shares), and Cameroon (240 shares). There was a corresponding reduction in the amount of arrears related to these subscriptions (ADB/ADF, Board of Governors, *Annual Report* 1985:68). Egypt introduced another potentially explosive issue at the 1984 board of governors' meeting. According to the compromises worked out upon admission of the extraregionals, the regionals retained a mandatory two-thirds of their voting power. With the escalating arrears problem and the voting penalties invoked for failure to pay, the regionals' share of total votes could possibly be less than the proportion required by statute. Given this possibility and the acute sensitivity of the regionals to the Africanicity requirement, the sanctions for nonpayment may become so unacceptable to regional members that they try to modify the decision making process within the institution, a move that would exacerbate the regional versus extraregional cleavage.

The ADB possesses four potentially potent techniques of influence. The most general is that the ADB is a conveyor of economic ideas to member states; through ideas, the IGO influences state members. This technique of ADB influence is of only recent origin, although the potential long-term impact of the marketplace of ideas may be considerable. Historically in the ADB, loan preconditions have been the most direct approach, as preconditions legally tie the borrowers before disbursement begins: disbursement does not proceed until preconditions are met to management's satisfaction. In contrast to the simplified preconditions found in loans issued by the international private banks, ADB preconditions have become more specific, tied to both management and policy decisions. Herein is the root of their weakness. Preconditions are tied to projects alone. In order to go beyond the project level, ADB officials increasingly discuss more general preconditions with national decision makers, but these general preconditions are unwritten. They affect the future disposition of loans, not current disbursement.

The ADB, like other international financial institutions, is moving toward more general conditionalities, including provision of economic advice not specifically tied to projects. Although non-project lending is currently limited by statute, discussion of the country's macroeconomic policies is increasingly integral to the loan negotiating process both for non-project sectoral/program lending and specific projects. The advice given as part of nonbinding conditionalities emphasizes market decentralization and increased use of market pricing similar to IMF conditionalities, but is less precise, more flexible, and most importantly, nonbinding. The imposition of such conditionalities makes the negotiating process between the state member and the lending organization more complex and more attenuated.

Likewise, sanctions are a potent instrument that the ADB has increasingly utilized to try to force payment of arrears by imposing various levels of punishment for states' failure to pay. Since the imposition of automatic sanctions is a relatively new phenomenon, it is premature to assess its impact on national policy, beyond concluding that some countries have paid up after sanctions. The ongoing contentious debates within the executive council over the propriety of sanctions suggest that such coercive measures will never be a permanent technique of ADB influence. Sensitive to charges of manipulation by major extraregional donors, the ADB has been walking a tightrope between the necessity to ensure economic viability through repayment and cautious use of threatening sanctions.

The ADB possesses unique capabilities to influence states. Not only has it mustered economic resources, but it has earned political legitimacy. As Edward C. Wolf of Worldwatch Institute reported at the 1986 U.S. House of Representative hearings, "Given the Bank's African character, the likelihood that its recommendations will be taken seriously by African pol-

icymakers is enhanced" (1986:11). One of the potential liabilities for the ADB of imposing stricter loan preconditions,
tightening and enforcing conditionalities, and advocating
stronger sanctions for arrears is increased risk that the organization will be viewed as politically tainted. As the ADB moves in
the more controversial policy directions outlined above, we may
expect the myth of political neutrality to be permanently dis-
pelled. Influencing national policy decisions means that the
ADB becomes a political actor in the borrowing country. By
becoming a political actor and losing its aura of technical neutrality, the ADB may be more constrained by policy choices
available.

The Constraints on
ADB Influence

The African Development Bank is constrained in its actions. Three types of constraints—environmental, organizational, and political—are particularly salient. These constraints alter the patterns of decision making within the organization despite the promises of the founding agreement. They affect the ability of state participants to agree to and support coherent policies. They set the parameters for loan negotiations and project implementation. And these constraints may determine the choice of ADB techniques to influence borrowers' policies and the effectiveness of the technique selected.

All African international organizations including the African Development Bank are constrained by a suite of environmental problems. First, the geographic, economic, and political diversity found in Africa means that for organizations whose interests are continental, policies must be tailored to a variety of often-changing conditions. The geographic expansiveness of Sudan or Zaire contrasts with the ministates of Equitorial Guinea or Gambia. The dryness of the Sahelian countries contrasts with the tropical rain forests of the Congo basin states. The oil-generated wealth found in Libya or Algeria is contrasted with the poverty found in Guinea Bissau or Burkina Faso. And the political divisions of fifty-one independent governments, some only a sovereign country in name, mean that international organizations in Africa deal with a minimum of fifty-one different governments and fifty-one different economic systems.

Second, these geographic differences and distances combined with the undeveloped stated of infrastructure mean that reliability and timeliness of communication are significant constraints. Poor internal communications within borrowing countries and between the countries and the executive board have limited ADB's operations. Written communication within Africa takes three to four weeks and telephone lines are slow and unreliable, often nonexistent in project areas. Interstate air transport is expensive and intracountry transport glacially slow and uncomfortable. These communication weaknesses play havoc with the project cycle, slowing down lending timetables. Projects in East Africa and in particularly isolated areas are especially affected. Unfortunately, the ADB's regional offices located in Harare, Nairobi, and Yaoundé have not fully resolved the problem and administrative decentralization is costly.

Third, the well-documented instability of African governments suggests that ADB's interactions with specific regimes may be short lived, and hence ADB's techniques of influence are more difficult to implement. As one official describes, every time there is a change of regime, each of the new ministers takes at least six months to evaluate the commitments of their predecessors. During that reevaluation, while the tasks under contract may continue, all paperwork concerning the next phases comes to a grinding halt, including authorizations for repayment of loans.

At the project level, governmental instability slows the process. Loans not yet signed may be reviewed to evaluate whether the preconditions are compatible with "new" directions of policy. Direct policy advice offered, especially unwritten suggestions that might condition future disposition of loans, is forgotten in the bureaucratic shuffle. Consistent ADB policy advice is undermined by the radical policy changes often accompanying unplanned regime change. Thus government instability complicates and retards the ADB process. As Leon Gordenker found for the United Nations Development Program (UNDP) in Africa, "the unstable situation also tended to endanger past accomplishments and threaten future performance, even while it made a triumph of decentralization over any

centralized control or influence on the multilateral agences"
(1976:172-73). And the ADB is no exception.

Fourth, economic weaknesses and administrative poor management within the African countries present another set of
environmental constraints. The most glaring obstacle until recently has been lack of funds. The ADB was founded as a bank to
provide financing by collectively the world's poorest set of nations for the world's poorest countries. Economic resources
were admittedly scarce, with income barely sufficient to cover
administrative costs as discussed in chapter 2. Although the
Bank has the economic resources since the admission of the
extraregionals in the 1980s, many regional states are in arrears
or appear incapable of absorbing available funds.

Fifth, development planning systems within national governments are characteristically weak. Such agencies lack both
adequate statistics and skilled personnel. Particularly weak in
ADB's opinion are the national development banks with their
bureaucracies tightly linked to the state. ADB post hoc evaluations reveal that loans channeled through these banks have been
generally among the least effective. Rather than funneling
money for small projects in the private sector, they have been
used for pet projects of political figures, many of whom have
financial interests in the projects. Numerous small projects are
difficult to monitor and control.

The long-term goal of the ADB is to overcome some of these
environmental constraints both on the continent generally and
within borrowing countries. For example, multinational projects were given priority as described in chapter 4. It was envisioned that such projects would improve telecommunications
and roads between borrowing countries. Due to the political
instability of members and the difficulties in coordinating the
projects among national development planning agencies, however, fewer regional projects have been funded—too few to resolve the environmentally caused problems. These environmental constraints do not uniformly affect ADB projects.
Surprisingly, Ethiopia and Botswana have two of the best records
for implementation of ADB projects in spite of environmental
difficulties.

Organizational weaknesses within the ADB have also posed formidable constraints on its influence. One of the most basic issues, the bilingualism of the Bank and the perpetual push by the Arabs to force trilingualism, adds both time delays and expense to all communications and negotiations within the Bank and between the Bank and its members. Linguistic preference and capability, together with the substantive expertise of professionals working on a project or with certain governments, must always be considered in personnel placement. Hence the Bank has not always been able to assemble the most technically expert teams, but rather has favored teams composed of individuals possessing other qualifications, such as linguistic capabilities.

The many personnel problems discussed in chapter 2—including the dearth of macroeconomic experts, the stagnation in the personnel system, the difficulty of recruiting personnel from all geographic regions, and the need for a career service—all have acted as considerable constraints on the system. For example, the quality of personnel (judged in terms of educational credentials and practical experience) is a positive asset to the organization. Unfortunately, these same individuals function in a "clogged" promotion system. Recruitment for new positions is conducted outside rather than within the organization, making it difficult to move to new positions of responsibility or to change career tracks. Efforts by the Bank to move into non-project lending have been thwarted by this stagnant system. Bank management has demanded new appointments, including experts in sectoral lending and macroeconomists trained to give policy advice. However, new staffing requests have been rejected by the executive directors in order to contain administrative expenses. What the staff has not done is rotate competent personnel into these new areas and provide additional training to compensate for educational deficiencies. In addition, the formal and informal restrictions on hiring permanent extraregional staff are an underlying personnel problem, particularly because many of the extraregional executive directors view the addition of such personnel as necessary to the implementation of the new functions of the organization.

Although money may be readily available for viable projects, other economic constraints persist. The problem of arrears seriously undermines the financial strength of the organization, particularly because the ADB is the most closely scrutinized by the international financial community of the multilateral development banks. Even if the funds are available, the ADB lacks economic expertise in some areas of non-project lending/sectoral loans. Hence, non-project lending is often conducted with the World Bank as the lead cofinancing institution.

These deficiencies in organization have repercussions on both the loans made and projects completed. No consensus emerges on what stage of the loan process is the weakest. Some ADB administrators and government personnel insist that the project identification stage is a bottleneck. The inability of governments to identify viable projects and to finance preinvestment studies and ADB's inability to aid the countries with more economic and technical assistance at this critical stage result in the bottleneck. The current dearth of economically viable projects in the pipeline attests to this weakness.

Disbursement problems have also been cited as a critical weakness in the organization (Kidder, Peabody and Co., 1984; Price Waterhouse, 1977). The high percentage of nondisbursed money found under Bank control may be attributed to one or more of the following interpretations. First, low disbursement may reflect the inefficiency of the organization. ADB officials cannot administratively handle the volume of resources they have at their disposal. Second, low disbursement rates may reflect a purposive management strategy. As a new and African institution, the ADB is highly scrutinized by the international money markets; thus, more than other institutions, the Bank may be forced to be more conservative by carrying higher reserves to verify its creditworthiness (Friedman, 1984). Third, low disbursements may result from the fact that many African countries cannot afford to borrow on the Bank's terms—a basic interest rate of 9.86% plus 2% in commission and commitment fees; hence most nonconcessionary funds go to the more-developed countries like Kenya, Zimbabwe, Ivory Coast, or Cameroon (Blackburn, 1985:14). These countries are limited by the absorptive capacity of their economies. Fourth, disbursements may lag because the governments have not been prompt in meeting the numerous preconditions prior to first disbursement. Changes in regime have delayed government submission of appropriate documents during the project cycle necessary for disbursement; and ADB loan officers covering between fifteen and twenty-five projects cannot hope to meet all demands for disbursement in a timely fashion.

In 1985 and 1986 there were dramatic increases in disbursement rates, largely due to efforts by ADB officials to strengthen the dialogue with governmental officials directly responsible for project execution. As a result, in 1985 there was a 27.06% increase in disbursements (ADB/ADF, Board of Governors, *Annual Report*, 1985:69). Yet although disbursement problems may delay project implementation, in general, they do not affect the outcome of well-conceived and well-executed projects.

Supervision of projects was mentioned the most often as the major weakness in the ADB lending cycle. According to ADB officials, poor supervision leading to poor execution of projects stems from a lack of specialized personnel. Loan officers and country economists cover too many countries. The remoteness of sites and poor communications make constant supervision all the more problematic. Some officials admit that ADB responsibles visit project sites twice—at initiation and upon completion, not the four times a year written in the contracts. Yet in countries lacking technical workers, supervision is the best insurance for guaranteeing quality projects.

Finally post-evaluation studies have been cited as a weak link in the lending process. Although such studies are conducted, they tend to evaluate solely the performance of the Bank in the project, not the broader questions of viability of the project, impact on the target groups, or contribution of the project to national economic development. Most critically, these studies, even the compact summaries, are not widely circulated (the contractors are not even on the list) and in the hurried bureaucratic environment common in organizations like the ADB, more pressing matters take precedent. Institutional practices clearly exacerbate "weak links" in the project process, links that result in suboptimal projects completed under ADB auspices.

Perhaps the most intriguing of ADB's weaknesses is its lack of a clearly enunciated theory of economic development. Officials, although largely trained in the tradition, have eschewed becoming too closely identified with the liberal economic approach, a development strategy that places a high premium on unleashing the private enterprise sector to maximize economic gain in an unfettered, uncontrolled international market. But ADB economists have, with equal reluctance, stayed away from a statist approach associated with the more radical economic development perspective. Recent papers written by the Policy and Planning Department have taken preliminary steps to integrate the two perspectives (ADB, Planning and Research Department, 1984b).

It is unclear, however, whether the lack of a specified theory of economic development hinders or actually facilitates ADB interactions with borrowing states. Both sides of the argument are plausible. On the one hand, a consistent view of economic development by the Bank would permit states to propose projects more closely adhering to the guidelines of the theory, perhaps hastening the project identification/appraisal phase. Lending to the ADB may then be augmented, assuming that lenders find the theory acceptable. On the other hand, failure to develop such a theory may give the ADB more flexibility and hence more legitimacy. In contrast to the World Bank and IMF, which are unequivocally associated with the liberal theory of economic development, a more pragmatic ad hoc approach, ambiguously called "appropriate to the African context," may expedite state acceptance and reduce political controversy. A pragmatic approach may then reflect the distinct development needs of a borrowing state, rather than a preordained theory of economic development.

The lack of administrative efficiency generally means that the project cycle will be attenuated, that all countries will negotiate more with generalists rather than with macroeconomic experts, and that fewer projects will be completed. But these weaknesses in the ADB administrative system are certainly not unique to the ADB, even though several personnel suggested that were pecularily African shortcomings.

Political constraints comprise the last category of limitations on the ADB. Such constraints emanate from donors, borrowers, and ADB management.

The ADB is "ripe" for *political* conflict, for as one American official described: "all divisions are reflected in the institution"— francophones vs. anglophones vs. arabophones; Arabs vs. non-Arabs; regional vs. extraregional members; East Africans vs. West Africans; technocrats vs. generalists. In such diverse international organizations, both formal rules and informal procedures are devised to guarantee that various constituencies receive relatively equal treatment. Certain conventions must be followed to respect political sensitivities and minimize conflict.

One of the most important of these conventions concerns the allocation of loans. To ensure the presence of the Bank in all countries, each African country, large or small, is "entitled" to one fundable project every year. Beyond that entitlement, funds are allocated by an unspecified formula encompassing relative economic deprivation, differences in size of population, and relative absorptive capacities of national economies.

Table 7 shows actual distribution of loans by states. Between 1974 and 1986, the goal of one project per country per year has not been met. Zaire received thirty-one loans; Djibouti, three; Sao Tomé and Principe, three; Angola, three; and Algeria, four. An examination of the whole time period reveals that cumulative amount of funding has also varied considerably from Djibouti's $15.9 million to $356.8 million for Zaire and over $200 million for both Egypt and Tunisia. As more sanctions for arrears are imposed and states are not permitted to borrow (see chapter 5), the allocation system for loans is apt to become further skewed from the criteria outlined above. States not receiving what governments perceive to be their fair share of loans are dissatisfied.

Dissatisfaction has also risen about the regional distribution of loans. As a political institution, the ADB also tries to be

Table 7. African Development Bank Group, Effective Loans by
          Country, 1974-86

Country	Total $'000	Number of Loans
Algeria	21,166	4
Angola	52,135	3
Benin	102,926	20
Botswana	158,737	17
Burkina Faso	83,799	11
Burundi	157,427	21
Cameroon	121,096	16
Cape Verde	36,104	9
Central African Republic	79,715	14
Chad	39,331	6
Comoros	56,924	8
Congo	90,876	13
Djibouti	15,962	3
Egypt	229,985	18
Equatorial Guinea	23,553	7
Ethiopia	238,776	22
Gabon	123,253	11
Gambia	67,960	13
Ghana	184,582	19
Guinea	126,299	18
Guinea Bissau	57,861	11
Ivory Coast	156,416	14
Kenya	117,420	15
Lesotho	138,881	21
Liberia	125,630	17
Madagascar	132,096	12
Malawi	155,679	19
Mali	129,663	20
Mauritania	62,683	14
Mauritius	43,917	10
Morocco	175,341	15
Mozambique	142,851	17
Niger	108,629	16
Nigeria	9,832	2
Rwanda	107,472	19

Table 7. (continued)

Country	Total $'000	Number of Loans
Sao Tomé and Principe	9,759	3
Senegal	103,380	18
Seychelles	39,681	8
Sierra Leone	47,341	11
Somalia	95,691	15
Sudan	78,681	10
Swaziland	83,100	17
Tanzania	135,165	21
Togo	61,377	12
Tunisia	271,175	22
Uganda	129,853	14
Zaire	356,876	31
Zambia	173,315	17
Zimbabwe	107,227	8
Multinational		
East Africa	17,057	2
West Africa	113,117	16
Total	5,497,772	

Source: African Development Bank, Planning and Research Department. *Compendium of Statistics* (1987).

sensitive to regional differences. Table 8 shows the regional distribution of loans between 1979 and 1986. The data are difficult to compare because the number of countries in each region varies and the categories changed in 1982. But essentially, the percentage of funding going to Central Africa and North Africa has increased, while both East and West African shares have declined. The discrepancy is particularly great considering that the east and west regions have the greatest number of individual states, albeit small ones. To quell criticism of regional disparities and favoritism, ADB has attempted to equalize these differences in funding levels among regions.

So, to a limited extent, concern for proportional distribution both among states and among regions affects lending patterns in

Table 8. Regional Distribution of Bank Group Loans, 1979-86 (%)

	1979	1980	1981	1982	1983	1984	1985	1986
Central Africa 11 countries + multinational	17.11	19.51	22.76	21.37	26.89	6.63	20.05	27.26
North Africa 7 countries + multinational[1]	13.17	11.76	20.53	11.29	9.01	23.71	34.64	34.52
West Africa 15 countries + multinational[2]	28.56	25.58	17.26	28.45	21.62	30.11	17.44	19.93
East Africa 17 countries + multinational	41.16	43.15	39.45	—	—	—	—	—
East Africa 9 countries	—	—	—	17.07	26.69	15.94	13.06	11.31
Southern Africa 8 countries	—	—	—	21.82	15.79	23.61	14.81	6.98

[1]Algeria stopped borrowing in 1978; Libya has never borrowed.
[2]Nigeria stopped borrowing in 1974.
Source: ADB/ADF, Board of Governors. *Annual Reports* (1984, 1986).

terms of the number of projects allocated to specific countries, the amount of such loans, and the regional distribution of loans.

These same concerns with country and regional representation affect the operation of the secretariat, particularly the selection of the president as described in chapter 2. However, as in other international organizations, selection of other secretariat personnel is governed by both technical qualifications and attention to equitable geographic distribution.

Table 9 shows the numbers of secretariat personnel from various countries over a representative three-year period 1981-83. At the professional level, West African recruits are disproportionately represented, fifteen from Benin and Nigeria, eleven from Cameroon, ten from Senegal and Guinea, twenty-one from Ghana and the Ivory Coast, twelve from Mali, and thirteen from Togo. But Ethiopia with twelve professionals, Tanzania with fourteen, and Uganda and Zaire each with fifteen

Table 9. Structure of Bank Group Staff by Nationality, 1981-83

| Category | | | | | | | Supporting Staff | | | | | | | | |
| | Professional | | | Sub professional[1] | | | General service | | | Manual | | | Total | | |
Member Countries	1981	1982	1983	1981	1982	1983	1981	1982	1983	1981	1982	1983	1981	1982	1983
Algeria	4	4	4	—	—	—	—	—	—	—	—	—	4	4	4
Benin	10	14	15	4	3	3	16	18	19	2	2	2	32	37	39
Botswana	1	1	1	—	—	—	1	1	1	—	—	—	2	2	2
Burundi	1	2	1	—	—	1	1	1	—	—	—	2	2	3	2
Cameroon	7	10	11	6	5	6	17	15	14	2	1	1	32	31	32
Central African Republic	4	4	4	1	1	1	—	—	—	—	—	—	5	5	5
Chad	2	3	4	1	1	1	4	4	3	1	1	1	8	9	9
Comoros	—	—	—	—	—	—	—	—	1	—	—	—	—	—	1
Congo	6	9	9	1	1	1	3	2	2	2	2	2	12	14	14
Egypt	4	6	4	—	—	—	1	1	1	—	—	—	5	7	5
Ethiopia	11	12	12	1	1	1	6	5	5	—	—	—	18	18	18
Gabon	2	2	2	—	—	—	1	1	1	—	—	—	3	3	3
Gambia	1	1	1	—	—	—	3	3	4	—	—	—	4	4	5
Ghana	17	19	21	5	5	8	18	19	23	4	5	4	44	48	56
Guinea	8	9	10	2	2	2	12	12	14	7	7	7	29	30	33
Ivory Coast	13	17	21	5	5	5	96	101	114	42	41	48	156	164	188
Kenya	10	8	8	1	2	2	4	7	7	—	—	—	15	17	17
Lesotho	—	—	1	—	—	—	—	—	—	—	—	—	—	—	1
Liberia	4	4	6	1	1	1	2	2	2	—	—	—	7	7	9
Madagascar	3	3	5	—	—	—	—	—	—	—	—	—	3	3	5
Malawi	3	5	6	—	—	—	—	—	—	—	—	—	3	5	6
Mali	11	11	12	1	—	—	18	20	20	3	3	4	33	34	36
Mauritania	2	2	1	—	—	—	—	—	—	—	—	—	2	2	1
Mauritius	5	6	5	—	—	—	4	7	7	—	—	—	9	13	12
Morocco	7	7	8	—	—	—	2	1	1	—	—	—	9	8	9
Niger	—	1	1	—	—	—	2	1	1	1	1	1	3	3	3
Nigeria	15	16	15	4	4	4	27	29	27	4	4	4	50	53	50
Rwanda	3	2	4	—	—	—	—	—	—	—	—	—	3	2	4
Senegal	8	9	10	1	1	1	8	10	9	2	2	2	19	22	22
Sierra Leone	7	7	7	1	1	1	12	12	11	2	2	2	22	22	21
Somalia	6	6	6	—	—	—	—	—	—	—	—	—	6	6	6
Sudan	5	5	6	—	—	—	1	—	—	—	—	—	6	5	6
Tanzania	10	12	14	—	1	1	1	2	2	—	—	—	11	15	17

(continued)

Table 9. (continued)

Category	Professional			Sub professional[1]			General service			Manual			Total		
Member Countries	1981	1982	1983	1981	1982	1983	1981	1982	1983	1981	1982	1983	1981	1982	1983
Togo	11	11	13	2	2	6	21	22	19	2	3	3	36	38	41
Tunisia	6	7	9	1	2	2	1	1	1	—	—	—	8	10	12
Uganda	10	12	15	—	—	—	5	5	5	—	—	—	15	17	20
Upper Volta	4	5	5	1	1	1	17	18	19	33	30	32	55	54	57
Zaire	14	14	15	1	1	1	2	2	3	1	1	1	18	18	20
Zambia	3	4	4	1	1	1	—	—	1	1	1	—	5	6	6
Zimbabwe	—	1	2	—	—	—	—	—	—	—	—	—	—	1	2
Subtotal	238	271	298	41	41	49	306	322	338	109	106	114	694	740	799
Other															
Canada	—	—	—	—	—	—	—	—	1	—	—	—	—	—	1
France	2	2	2	—	—	—	—	—	2	—	—	—	2	2	3
Germany	—	—	—	—	—	—	—	—	1	—	—	—	—	—	1
Italy	1	1	—	—	—	—	—	—	—	—	—	—	1	1	—
Subtotal	3	3	2	—	—	—	—	—	3	—	—	—	3	3	5
Total	241	274	300	41	41	49	306	322	341	109	106	114	697	743	804

[1]This category was created in 1976.

Source: ADB Planning and Research Department. *Compendium of Statistics* (1984).

have a disproportionate share as well. At both the general service and manual level, citizens of host Ivory Coast and its neighbors (Ghana and Guinea) have received the most positions. Ivorian personnel are increasingly bilingual, and Guinea and Ghana represent the two major language groups. Relative to population size and economic contributions, the Arab-speaking North is underrepresented.

Member governments constantly lobby ADB recruiters to hire more nationals from their particular countries, trying to balance substantive needs and technical qualifications. But the need to hire from a geographically large and diverse constituency has not yet erupted into a major political issue, except under the controversial President Fordwor, who was accused of hiring too many Ghanaians.

Political considerations of the donor extraregional members also constrain the operations of the African Development Bank. Of primary concern to the donors is procurement. According to most of the extraregional executive directors, a major motivation for their participation in the ADB is to try to increase that country's share of procurement from loan contracts. One of the main tasks of the executive directors is to communicate information about procurement possibilities to appropriate governmental authorities and, in some instances, to private-sector officials. Hence some of the smaller donors do not extensively participate in the loan negotiation process. What happens after loan approval is of greater importance to them.

Table 10 shows the breakdown in procurement. France and French companies are the overwhelming beneficiaries, with over 20% of procurement in 1983 and 18.98% in 1986. The historic colonial ties forged by France and their record in training African technical experts used to working with products manufactured in the former colonial power mean that when contracts are let, they are often written expressly for French equipment using French specifications. In addition, the French government, more than any other donor government, plays a critical role (makes a "monumental effort" in the words of one) to support French enterprise by helping them to receive procurement. For example, the French ambassador will often shepherd business leaders around and help them to make the necessary contacts. The French record of procurement success and the energy expended to obtain procurement is rather ironic considering that country's initial reticence to participate in the African Development Bank group. The fear that other extraregionals would replace French economic interests and business ties was evidently an unfounded one.

In 1986 the Federal Republic of Germany supplanted Great Britain as the second largest recipient of procurement contracts, 10.86% and 9.33%, respectively. In contrast, relative to the size of contributions, both the United States and Japan's record of procurement is unimpressive, 4.23% and 3.39%, respectively.

Table 10. Procurement of Goods and Services on African
        Development Bank Group Loans by Country of
        Origin, 1983, 1986 (cumulative %)

Country	Bank group	
	1983 (%)	1986 (%)
Argentina	0.01	0.02
Australia	0.01	—
Austria	0.66	.40
Belgium	4.28	4.09
Brazil	0.46	.49
Canada	1.09	1.07
China (Formosa)	0.12	.11
Denmark	0.91	.72
Finland	0.20	.19
France	20.19	18.98
Germany (Dem. Rep.)	0.04	.02
Germany (Fed. Rep.)	9.98	10.86
Great Britain	10.10	9.33
Greece	0.02	.01
Holland	1.51	1.42
Hong Kong	—	.01
Hungary	0.01	—
India	0.36	.30
Ireland	0.01	.02
Israel	0.08	.04
Italy	8.18	8.30
Japan	3.14	3.39
Korea (South)	0.19	.67
Luxemburg	0.25	.20
Malaysia	0.01	.01
Norway	0.08	.34
Poland	0.03	.02
Portugal	0.75	.89
Spain	0.36	.35
Sweden	0.87	.83
Switzerland	2.37	2.19
United States	5.09	4.23
Yugoslavia	0.65	.80
Regional Members	27.98	29.71

Source: African Development Bank Planning and Research Department. *Compendium of Statistics* (1984, 1987).

The executive directors from these two countries see that one of their primary tasks is to remedy the situation. Although the lack of Japanese involvement and experience in Africa is a difficult obstacle to overcome, the Japanese government is intervening directly, following the French model. Anglophone countries have tapped the United States, Great Britain, and Canada for procurement. Canadian companies have the advantage of being able to recruit francophone speakers. But neither American nor British companies have been helped in procuring contracts by their respective governments. Both the British government (for lack of funds) and the American government (to maintain an arms' length relationship with business) have remained relatively uninvolved in procurement activities.

One of the opportunities that the United States has had to receive a larger share of procurement is through U.S. Agency for International Development (USAID) contracts awarded to ADB. USAID has funded prefeasibility studies for the Bank, paid technical assistants working at headquarters, operated training institutes, and provided some "commodities," namely computer equipment and systems for ADB/Abidjan. With an additional USAID grant of $15 million made in 1985 to the ADB, total USAID contributions since 1968 have reached $28.5 million. These funds require purchases of American-made products.

Of secondary concern to the donors is employment of technical experts. The ADB has been generally reluctant to accept any extraregional technical experts, even though these personnel are funded by the extraregionals and are under fixed-term appointments. Not until the mid-1980s did the Bank consider hiring extraregionals on a permanent basis. Table 11 presents the figures on extraregional technical assistants. There are so few extraregional technical experts that the comparisons among the countries are not very meaningful. But in all cases, extraregional executive directors have pushed the organization to hire more permanent personnel from extraregional countries and to expand the technical assistance program. Unfortunately, the Bank has not always employed these personnel in jobs commensurate with their expertise, experience, and expecta-

Table 11. Technical Assistance Experts by Country of Origin

	1973	1974	1975	1976	1977	1978	1979
Multilateral Technical Assistance							
FAO	2	2	1	1	1	1	1
UNDP	4	3	5	3	—	—	—
Bilateral Technical Assistance							
Belgium	1	1	—	1	2	2	2
Brazil	—	—	—	—	—	—	—
Canada	—	—	—	—	2	2	—
Denmark	—	—	—	—	—	—	—
Fed. Rep. of Germany	2	2	2	1	2	2	1
Finland	—	—	1	1	1	1	1
France	—	—	—	—	—	—	—
India	—	—	—	—	—	—	—
Italy	—	—	1	1	1	—	—
Japan	—	1	1	—	1	1	1
Netherlands	1	1	—	—	—	—	1
Norway	1	1	2	1	1	3	2
Sweden	—	1	1	1	2	1	2
Switzerland	—	—	1	1	—	3	4
United Kingdom	—	2	1	2	2	1	4
United States of America	2	1	1	—	—	1	4
Yugoslavia	—	—	1	1	1	1	1
Total	13	15	18	14	16	20	24

tions. They have been largely limited to "training" regional secretariat personnel. Yet because these individuals command two to three times the salary of the secretariat officials and their responsibilities have been perfunctory, they are not always well received.

At the most general level, some donors, particularly the United States, are concerned with the content of decisions made at the ADB. As examined above, although the United States does not have the legal authority to veto decisions, as a major donor it does take the opportunity to try to ensure that decisions which the ADB makes are congruent with policies it

Table 11. (continued)

	1980	1981	1982	1983	1984	1985	1986
Multilateral Technical Assistance							
FAO	1	—	—	—	—	—	—
UNDP	—	—	—	—	—	—	—
Bilateral Technical Assistance							
Belgium	2	3	4	3	2	3	3
Brazil	—	—	—	—	—	2	—
Canada	—	3	3	4	2	4	3
Denmark	—	1	1	3	3	4	2
Fed. Rep. of Germany	1	1	2	1	1	—	—
Finland	1	1	2	2	1	1	2
France	1	2	2	2	1	6	6
India	—	—	—	—	1	2	1
Italy	1	3	3	1	2	2	2
Japan	—	—	1	1	—	—	—
Netherlands	2	—	—	1	—	—	—
Norway	1	2	3	1	1	—	1
Sweden	3	—	—	—	3	3	3
Switzerland	4	3	4	1	1	2	4
United Kingdom	4	4	3	4	4	1	1
United States of America	5	4	3	1	3	3	1
Yugoslavia	—	—	—	—	—	—	—
Total	26	27	31	25	25	33	29

Note: No multilateral technical assistance was provided by the World Bank between 1973 and 1986. Source: African Development Bank Planning and Research Department. *Compendium of Statistics* (1984, 1987).

is following in the other multilateral development banks (see chapter 10) and are consistent with overall American foreign policy objectives. The other donors have been either reticent to view the ADB from this political perspective, or they have not bothered to do so. Even France, the one country with long-standing strategic, economic, and political interests on the continent (see Lellouche and Moisi, 1979; Mingst and Bon, 1980;

Staniland, 1987), has not tried overtly to influence the ADB other than on procurement issues.

Of the three types of constraints on the ADB—environmental, organizational, and political—the environmental ones probably affect most dramatically ADB's relationship with its members and ADB's overall performance. The ADB is, however, the least able to overcome this set of constraints. Rivalries among various groups of members, among borrowers contending for their share of loans or their share of representatives in the ADB bureaucracy, among donors for shares of procurement or for an opportunity to influence policies within the organization also present significant political constraints on the organization. These organizational weaknesses make the environmental constraints even more difficult to overcome. The ability of the ADB to influence state behavior alone is diminished. Hence ADB's relationship with other development organizations working in Africa is critical, the subject explored in chapters 7 and 8.

The ADB and
the World Bank

To promote economic development in member states, the African Development Bank has worked with numerous development organizations in Africa. These other organizations, both public intergovernmental organizations and nongovernmental groups (including private voluntary organizations and the international banks) are part of the environmental setting within which the ADB must operate. These organizations not only add to ADB's opportunities and ability to function by cofinancing projects and introducing new approaches to problems confronted, but they also pose constraints to the ADB. The Bank actively competes with these development agencies for the ear of borrowing governments, for funds furnished by the international financial community, for qualified African employees, and for viable projects to finance. Thus, because these organizations are involved in both cooperation and competition with each other, interorganizational politics results.

Interorganizational cooperation and conflict emanates from pressures arising from the constrained pattern of interdependence among organizations (Evan, 1978:84). Why interdependence occurs can be explained in several ways. The need for resources (money, a specialized skill) and the desire to add new specialties to the organization at reduced cost may propel organizations into interdependence (Aiken and Hage, 1978:181-82)—that is, organizations may find it in their mutual interest to enjoy a symmetrical, mutually beneficial relationship. Interdependency may also arise out of the need to innovate. Such organizations, faced with an uncertain environment, may innovate to exclude rivals (a likely source of conflict) or innovate by coordination and cooperation (Assetto, 1986). And interdependency is developed by organizations contending and vying for "linking-pin status," organizations desiring to be the node through which a network is loosely joined (Aldrich and Whetton, 1981; Jönsson, 1986). But the limited presence of scarce resources and the competition that follows may result in organizations in a dependent relationship (Aldrich, 1979:118-19), a relationship that is asymmetrical.

In this chapter, the basis of interorganizational politics between the World Bank and ADB is explored. What factors have propelled the WB and ADB into interdependency? How has the ADB tried to lessen its dependency on the WB since the 1980s? How has this affected interorganizational politics?

Cofinancing projects by international organizations in Africa is frequent. For example, in the eleven years between 1974 and 1984, the World Bank and ADB cofinanced a total of fifty-four projects; and in the program for the period 1984-87, twenty-two projects were cofinanced (ADB/ADF, Board of Governors, *Annual Report* 1984). The need for cofinancing stems from the weaknesses in African governments examined in chapter 6, including governmental instability, weak development planning institutions lacking adequate statistical bases, and overtly political national development banks. This results in the inability of many governments to identify viable projects and satisfy conditions for counterpart financing independently.

The process of cofinancing reinforces an unstated hierarchy among the organizations, a hierarchy based on longevity, experience, and material resources. Some of the economic development organizations have been long-time actors in development, particularly the World Bank and the United Nations' Economic Commission for Africa (ECA), whereas others are either new or have only recently acquired sufficient economic resources to make an impact, such as the African Development Bank. The smaller regional economic organizations, such as the Conseil de l'Entente, Economic Community of West African States (ECO-

WAS), and the West African Economic Community (CEAO) lack both professional expertise and contributions by extraregional donors. So almost immediately, in a continent crowded with IGOs, there is a potential hierarchy, with the older, internationally financed at the apex and the smaller, regionally financed, often understaffed organizations at the bottom of this hypothetical pyramid. Such a hierarchy is reinforced by the movement of African personnel within these organizations. Being uniformly trained in West European and North American institutions of higher learning, an individual's initial experience may be at the "up-start" less-prestigious local organizations; the more aggressive and presumably the more qualified are promoted up through the hierarchy, often leading to World Bank employment. Hence the historical and resource predominance of the World Bank as premier capital financing institution in Africa is reinforced by a highly trained professional staff, "lifted" from other development organizations. This unspoken but acknowledged hierarchy is one of the ingredients of inter-organizational politics.

The basis for both potential conflict and cooperation between the WB and the other African-based economic development institutions is their inequality. There has been a tendency for the most prestigious, the WB, to be awarded the best projects. Projects rejected by the World Bank are then submitted to institutions lower on the organizational hierarchy. Prior to the 1980s the ADB did not have sufficient funds to be a viable competitor for projects. However, with the admission of extraregional members in 1982 and the substantial increase in capital resources that they brought, the ADB has the resources to disburse, making it a competitor in national capitals for scarce personnel and counterpart funds. For the first time in a continent in need of massive development financing and having institutions possessing these resources, there are more available funds than *viable* projects. The banks, to maintain disbursement levels and attractive project portfolios in order to obtain additional funds, scramble for the better projects. This creates an intense competition among financing institutions, one that may have beneficial effects for state recipients. Thus these two peculiarities, accentuated in Africa more than other parts of the Third World, provide the setting for attenuated interorganizational politics. And this interaction has both conflictual and cooperative undertones.

In the 1980s the World Bank has made a firm commitment to the economic development of Africa. Between 1982 and 1986, it disbursed $4,383.7 million to African countries, 19% of all WB expenditures. In contrast Latin American (Caribbean) and European-Middle Eastern countries each received 15% of WB funds; South Asia, 30%; and East Asia and Pacific, 20% (World Bank, *Annual Report* 1986). Additionally, in July 1985 the World Bank established the Special Facility for Sub-Saharan Africa with resources of $1.2 billion. The Special Facility is designed to help ease the adjustment process for countries that have already undertaken policy reform programs. In 1986 the Bank approved the allocation of $782 million to fifteen countries (World Bank, *Annual Report* 1986:22; World Bank, 1986).

The World Bank has been involved in the African debt issue of the 1980s. In an effort to moderate the debt crisis in specific countries, it initiated long-term structural adjustment lending. By early 1986, the World Bank had made nine structural adjustment loans in six African countries, with nine more being negotiated. Two indicators confirm the World Bank's commitment to Africa. Approximately 80% of the Bank's policy-based lending is in Africa—a twofold increase since the late 1970s. To administer these programs, the WB has stationed twenty-four resident representatives in Africa, more than in any other region (Callaghy, 1987:160-62; World Bank, *Annual Report* 1986).

Political differences between the WB and the ADB emerge from both theoretical orientations and practical considerations. The World Bank and the ADB do not share the same theory of economic development; indeed, the two institutions differ over whether having such a theory is necessary and useful. Not surprisingly, the policy approaches emerging from their respective theories are different.

The theory of economic development propounded by the World Bank for Africa in the 1980s was originally presented in

Accelerated Development in Sub-Saharan Africa: An Agenda for Action (World Bank, 1981a), a document that purportedly elucidated a fresh approach to African development by the WB. The report attributes poor economic performance to both internal structural problems (undeveloped human resources, economic disruption following decolonization) and external factors (high energy prices, slow growth of world trade). Both factors have been exacerbated by domestic policy inadequacies, specifically trade and exchange-rate policies that have overprotected industry and stifled agriculture, administrative constraints from an overextended public sector, and a consistent bias against agriculture in terms of pricing, taxing, and exchange rate policies. Emanating from this analytical assessment of the problem are certain policies that during the 1980s formed the core of the World Bank's development approach.

Based on the World Bank's diagnosis of the "problem," a package of policy proposals was developed. To alleviate the trade/exchange-rate problem, the World Bank recommends that overvalued exchange rates must be corrected, price incentives improved for exports and domestic agriculture, tariff protection for industry lowered, and direct government controls reduced. Reform of parastatals is recommended by creating incentives for their more efficient performance and liquidation of inefficient performers. And industrial development should focus on increased incentives for indigenous entrepreneurship. To achieve these changes, non-project lending by the World Bank, as implemented through the Special Facility for Sub-Saharan Africa, is viewed as an essential instrument. Such funds can pay for the foreign exchange costs of imports and can be used for rehabilitation of projects already in place.

In 1984 the World Bank in its statement *Toward Sustained Development* reiterated its position that domestic policy reforms are essential for African development, but this time emphasized how donor-assistance strategies had often prevented such reforms. Proposals to increase donor coordination to remedy the problem were suggested. The report also placed more emphasis on long-term constraints to development, especially population growth. Thus although the two WB statements contained some different provisions, they did provide an explicit theory of African development and gave national decision makers a clear picture of policies and sectors that the World Bank would support.

In contrast, the African Development Bank has not published a coherent theory of economic development, as Bank officials acknowledge. Prior to the 1980s, the infant institution showed little recognition of the importance of theory guiding their project funding. The political requirements of funding at least one project in every member country every year propelled lending rather than an explicit theoretical framework did. However, with the publication of the Organization of African Unity's *Lagos Plan of Action* (1980), ADB personnel became "sensitized to this approach" and began to refer to the plan in economic research papers (ADB, Planning and Research Department, 1984a; 1984b).

Specifically, the Lagos Plan stresses African self-sufficiency in three broad sectors. Self-sufficient agricultural production is the first priority, as discussed in chapter 4. Energy is another priority sector. Short-term policies include creating a stable and guaranteed supply of oil to African countries, increased technical assistance to non-oil producers from African OPEC members, and concessionary prices for oil imports. In the longer term, policies focus on development of energy alternatives, including fossil fuels, hydropower, and nuclear capability. Finally, trade is viewed as critical, but the emphasis in the Lagos Plan of Action is on enhancing and diversifying intra-African trade leading to an African common market by the year 2000. A more ambiguous section of the Lagos Plan calls for restructuring monetary and financial institutions, with the eventual goal of integrating financial systems at the subregional level, but specific policies that would achieve the goal are not presented (Sesay, Ojo, and Fasehun, 1984). In sum, the Lagos Plan of Action aspires to African self-reliance. This general approach to economic development is, according to ADB officials, not official doctrine; the Bank's legitimacy may be threatened if policies reflect organizational doctrine rather than state needs.

In 1983 the ADB issued a joint paper with the Economic

Commission for Africa (ADB-ECA, 1983) in which both institutions acknowledged that Africa's problems were largely structural and required changes in national policies, including reforms in the public sector and guarantees of incentives for private initiatives. A close reading of the preconditions of ADB loan projects and policies advocated under implicit conditionality (chapter 5) suggest that these conditions are remarkably compatible with World Bank policies enunciated in *Accelerated Development* (World Bank, 1981a).

The funding priorities of ADB, however, have been in the agricultural sector, reflecting in part the Lagos Plan discussed in chapter 4. The ADB's movement into non-project lending as confirmed at President N'Diaye's swearing in at ADB's headquarters in 1985 permits countries to have potentially greater control over the financing received. Although non-project lending is currently limited to only 10% of all loans, it is and will be more closely tied to program lending, sectoral loans, and policy advice, loosely congruent with the Lagos Plan.

A potential conflict between the WB and ADB is evident concerning the utility of having an economic development theory in the first place. The World Bank contends that such a theory is an essential guide to lenders as well as a necessity to receive capital market funding, whereas the ADB's "loose adherence" to doctrine conforms to its belief that organizational legitimacy is enhanced if it is not too closely identified with a theoretical perspective. The contents of the respective theories do suggest differences in the types of policy instruments to be employed. These variations reflect differences in organizational ideologies—economic liberal orientation of the WB and in ADB's ideology much less specified. The ambiguity in ADB's "ideology" results from the fact that the preponderant economic staff have been academically trained in Western institutions and a neoclassical free market approach to development. But many, based on their prior experience in national government service, have become somewhat disillusioned with these precepts and more sensitive to a variety of national, "uniquely African" approaches to development. This internal tension within the organization may be another reason why the ADB has preferred not to outline a clear organizational ideology and has revealed only the barest sketches of a theory of economic development.

Interestingly enough, WB officials themselves have tended to dismiss the differences in orientation found in the *Agenda for Accelerated Development* and the *Lagos Plan of Action*. For example, the 1984 document *Toward Sustained Development* states, "Neither the essential objectives of African development nor the policy-issues that must be addressed to achieve them are in dispute, even though views on timing and priorities may differ" (1984:1). In fact, the WB has contended that the *Agenda* and *Lagos Plan* are really most complementary, with the former dealing with short- to medium-term responses to the economic and fiscal crisis and the latter dealing with long-term transformation of African economies (Gordon and Parker, 1984:9-12). Comparing these two documents, ADB officials perceive more differences. Although some ADB policies may be compatible with WB initiatives, as suggested by an examination of ADB conditionalities actually imposed, the speed with which the policies are implemented, the commitment that many African leaders feel to initiate politically explosive changes, and the obligatory character of the policies are questioned by the ADB. As one ADB official aptly summarized, most African countries do not want us "carrying the big stick." To preserve its organizational legitimacy, the ADB has opted for a more flexible timetable to implement policy reform and has sought accommodation to member states' national sensitivities.

The World Bank's *Accelerated Development* and the OAU's *Lagos Plan* have been the "lightning rods" for the ongoing debate on the relative importance of external and internal causes of African economic problems, with the OAU pointing to external problems and the World Bank to internal difficulties. Jennifer Seymour Whitaker suggests how both internal and external causes are linked. "[T]he skeins of causality are, finally, impossible to clearly disentangle. On the one hand, it seems clear that the macroeconomic policies of African governments, which discouraged exports, were a primary cause of Africa's declining trade shares. On the other hand, governmental policies responded to crises engendered by adverse external trends. In addition, declining maintenance of infrastructures and cutbacks in essential government services—at least in part the result of the foreign exchange shortfalls—eroded effective implementation of policy" (1986:3).

Differences in management approaches between the WB and ADB are also evident. These differences have inevitably occurred because the two organizations have never had access to the same amount of financial resources, competent personnel, or research facilities. Variances in management have arisen from the different demands placed on each institution from the international donors. For example, the World Bank not only has more resources at its disposal, but also it disperses a higher percentage of subscribed capital. The ADB has a high percentage of liquid assets to undisbursed loans, 70.4%, compared to the World Bank's 37.4% (Kidder, Peabody, 1984). This difference between the institutions in terms of their money management can be attributed to the fact that as a new *and* African institution, the ADB is highly scrutinized by the international money markets (Friedman, 1984).

Furthermore, differences between the two institutions in terms of representation in the field reinforces the World Bank's premier position. WB country missions help to identify projects; their twenty-four resident representatives provide continuous communication between the WB and country implementors of the project. The result is that the World Bank often gets the better projects—whereas in the graphic language of one, the ADB is the "garbage can," getting all the rejected WB projects. Although the description may be overdrawn, the fact is that the WB's physical presence gives it a strategic advantage. And this difference in management practice, derived in large part from the differential resource picture, creates the basis for ADB's and its personnel's sense of inferiority.

Differences in personnel policies and research facilities also accentuate the inequality. Relative to the WB, which employs one and often several economists for each borrowing country, the ADB lacks a sufficient number of professional personnel: three country economists cover twenty-five countries—such generalists cannot hope to become experts on all those countries. There is little mobility by personnel into these positions. And the research resources (libraries/data banks) that the ADB officials have at their disposal are vastly inferior to the facilities at the World Bank. What these inadequacies mean is that ADB "experts," while they may have considerable practical experience, need to rely on other data bases and other studies, more often than not on World Bank material.

These differences in management style based on differential in material resources have lead to a hierarchical relationship between the two organizations. With the WB having more resources and more experience, it is generally thrust into a "trainer" role. It is the WB that has taken the cofinancing lead. As officials describe the process, often World Bank officials conceive of a project; they find a "gap" in financing. They then ask the ADB to involve itself in that portion, partly as a way to "train" ADB officials. The WB has also seized the trainer role as it moves in new policy directions. For example, the WB, with its new emphasis on public sector/public enterprise rehabilitation loans and loans for non-project lending, asserts that the ADB does not have sufficient experience to work in these areas unassisted. Although ADB officials agree, conflict has arisen. For example, the ADB was assigned leader in a road maintenance project in Sierra Leone as part of its "training program," but the World Bank actually ended up with the lead position both through its own institutional aggressiveness and because of ADB shortcomings, particularly inflexible management of personnel. Under such circumstances, ADB's dependent position is reinforced.

Explanations for these institutional slippages may be more complex than just inefficient management. Some ADB officials suggest that they are explicitly "recoiling" from WB influence since their own financial resources have been secured. For example, the ADB has been increasingly reluctant to participate in joint institutes for training sponsored through the Economic Development Institute. A seminar on pricing was not attended officially by ADB personnel—a decision designed to affirm ADB autonomy, even though "unofficial" observers were sent.

Likewise, in the use of WB studies, ADB officials contend that such documents provide only the starting point for their own research. They are very sensitive to the accusation that ADB is merely duplicating WB research efforts. These symbolic gestures suggest that the ADB is trying to steer a more independent course.

Since there are policy differences between the two organizations on such issues as the obligatory nature of conditionality and on the superiority of the private sector, the ADB has chosen separation from the "father" institution. It may also be trying to install itself as link-pin organization in the African development financing network. The ability of an international organization to assume such a link-pin position is enhanced if it has multiple links, a high presence, low profile, asymmetric distribution of political expertise in its favor, and boundary role occupants in central positions (Jönsson, 1986:46). However, as the foregoing analysis has suggested, the World Bank has multiple links with key actors, a more pervasive physical presence, and greater political expertise. Thus, although the ADB may try to capitalize on its less prominent position, its ability to play a mediatory role is jeopardized by its less visible profile. Interviews conducted at ADB headquarters show that both secretariat members and state representatives desire the organization to play a mediatory role between African governments and donors, despite the resource and organizational asymmetry with the largest multilateral development institution.

Two conditions potentially augmenting ADB power vis-à-vis the WB are its physical location and the relative lack of pressure exerted by major donors. Location of World Bank headquarters in Washington, D.C., probably results in closer scrutiny of WB by American decision makers, and of course the weighted voting system guarantees a strong American position, as argued in chapter 10. The ADB in Abidjan is substantially removed from daily scrutiny by any of the major donors (the United States, Japan, Nigeria, Libya, and Egypt) and in contrast to the WB, American influence in terms of voting is relatively small. Since only two full-time American officials (ADB executive director/ alternate) are located at ADB headquarters, American influence is relatively subdued. As one interviewee commented, ADB's headquarters location guarantees the organization more freedom from hegemonic control than either the Inter-American Development Bank or WB has in Washington, D.C.

Despite this potential latitude, the final irony is that African countries themselves prevent the ADB from playing a more dominant role. Many states act to reinforce the hierarchical relationship between the World Bank and African Development Bank. Countries, according to officials in both institutions, tend to pay up loan arrears first to the World Bank and then to the ADB. African leaders are aware of the World Bank's greater resources and its greater potential to influence, and they believe that their "African brothers" will better understand their inability to pay. Under such conditions it is difficult for the ADB to establish itself as a linking-pin organization.

Conflictual tensions arising from differences in some aspects of economic development theory and management strategies are not the only outcomes of interorganizational politics. Cooperation between the two institutions exists. In this section the basis for this cooperation between two institutions having differential resources is explained. Each institution brings to the relationship a strength that the other lacks; hence, cooperation is facilitated.

The fact that the WB and ADB are both development institutions and banks leads to cooperation between these two institutions. They share common procedures and administrative approaches. Similarity of procedures facilitates interaction and is conducive to cooperation. The basic project cycle, the steps leading from the initial preinvestment survey, to appraisal, to project, disbursements, and post hoc evaluation is essentially the same. Cofinancing is easier under these circumstances. Hence, procedural congruence has enabled the two institutions to share in cooperative ventures.

Cofinancing of projects has been the most frequent outcome of these interactions. Between 1977 and 1982, ADB cofinanced an average of twenty projects a year (Gardiner and Pickett, 1984:103), mostly with the World Bank. This interaction is becoming increasingly institutionalized. For example, during a series of meetings held in January 1985, World Bank and ADB officials agreed to principles to guide aid coordination, including regular exchange of communications and the sharing of information on conditionalities. Specific cooperative ventures focus on the following areas:

a. Consultative Groups. The ADB wishes to be involved at earlier stages in the Consultative Group lending cycle, including the preparation of country economic reports leading to co-financing projects.
b. SAL/Sector Lending. The ADB wants to work closer with the WB to gain experience with non-project financing, specifically lending for sector rehabilitation. The ADB has been invited to participate in several SAL reviews, providing financing for expenditures in sectors within the framework of conditionalities defined by the WB.
c. Public Investment Review (PIR). World Bank staff briefs ADB officials on the utility and methodology of the PIR. Both institutions stress the need to coordinate their efforts in advising governments to prevent low return investments.
d. Technical Assistance. The two institutions need to concentrate their efforts on technical assistance for institution-building, in public enterprises rehabilitation, PIR implementation at the country level, and technical assistance on SAL-related work.
e. Economic/Sector Work. The WB is open to cooperate with ADB in economic and sector work, even given ADB's staff constraints and need to upgrade the economic analytical capabilities of its staff. Missions from the two banks should be jointly staffed. (World Bank, 1985)

Interaction opportunities between the two organizations are planned and institutionalized. Reciprocity with the expectation of gain is a crucial explanation for the relationship. The ADB is aware of its institutional weaknesses, its shortage of macro-economic experts, at a time when it is increasingly involved with non-project lending and offering policy advice. Forced to become an innovative organization by exigencies in the broader environment, the failure of economic development in Africa, the ADB has found it useful to cooperate with the more experienced World Bank. As both the World Bank and ADB innovate outside of project lending, the ADB, because of its legitimacy on the continent, serves as a buffer between the WB and its African constituency. To enhance ADB's success in this capacity, the WB has stated, it "understands" that there may be "disincentives" to ADB's involvement in all aspects of conditionality (World Bank, 1985).

The more the potential interactions, the more the opportunities for reciprocal exchanges, often culminating in cofinancing. As both ADB and WB innovate, the reciprocal basis for cooperation is enhanced. The ADB learns the intricacies and pitfalls of offering policy advice and of imposing implicit conditionalities and the WB tries to capitalize on ADB legitimacy by both cofinancing and coordinating common approaches to non-project lending. In other words, issue-specific factors have led to a convergence of perspectives facilitating cooperation.

Cooperation and conflict between the ADB and WB emerge from organization interdependence, with the ADB in a dependent position. The ADB is the newer organization, offering less prestigious employment possibilities; it has had fewer economic resources, and with that, a less-visible presence in the field. It has been "slower" to innovate, with the World Bank taking the lead in imposing conditionalities and suggesting policy reforms. ADB dependence is reinforced by the attitude of the African countries themselves, which have viewed the ADB as one of the "last lenders" and one of the "last to be repaid."

During the 1980s, the ADB has tried to extricate itself from its inferior position, "to steer the bank out of the shadow of the World Bank and International Monetary Fund" (Thurow, 1989:1), a viable strategy only after the adhesion of the extra-regional members and the augmentation of financial resources. The ADB became "sensitized" to the Lagos Plan, adopting some policy orientations that reflected a different ideological and policy orientation than that supported by the World Bank. Although the differences from the World Bank are not profound, the ADB orientation is more compatible with that of most African states. With this impetus, the ADB has tried to disassociate itself, at least symbolically, from the World Bank, hoping to be the linking-pin organization on the continent.

Loosening of the dependency relationship has positively affected interorganizational relations, the ADB being more willing to try innovative policies, even, in some cases, World Bank-inspired policies, and the World Bank increasingly viewing the ADB as a potential legitimizing agent for the multilateral development banks and for economic development institutions more generally.

The ADB and Other Development Institutions

African Development Bank's interactions with the World Bank have been most frequent for the reasons elaborated in chapter 7. Table 12 reports ADB's cofinancing activities for 1985 and 1986. ADB cofinancing with the World Bank comprised 25% and 29% of the total cofinanced projects in 1985 and 1986, respectively. More revealing of the magnitude of the WB and ADB relationship is the fact that these projects accounted for 60% and 57%, respectively, of the funds disbursed in cofinanced projects during the two years.

Likewise, ADB's relationships with other financiers are becoming more extensive. For example, during 1984 ADB officials had meetings with and/or signed cooperation arrangements leading to cofinancing with the following organizations (ADB/ADF, Board of Governors *Annual Report* 1985:40-42): Food and Agriculture Organization (FAO), eleven identification and sixteen joint preparation missions; International Civil Aviation Organization (ICAO), advisory and executing agency for ADB projects; Islamic Development Bank (ISDB), financing preinvestment and feasibility studies in common countries; International Fund for Agricultural Development (IFAD), eight cofinanced projects, joint institute for agricultural management training; United Nations Development Program (UNDP), beginning of systematic consultations; United Nations Educational, Scientific and Cultural Organization (UNESCO), joint project identification; United Nations Industrial Development

Table 12. Cofinancing of African Development Bank Group
Loans by Financier (in millions of dollars)

	1985		1986	
	Bank group amount	Total operations	Bank group amount	Total operations
ABEDA	19.99	3	—	—
AFESD	—	—	54.66	1
BDEAC	—	—	5.63	1
Belgium	4.42	1	18.84	1
BOAD	3.55	1	4.53	1
CCCE	57.20	3	53.05	2
CDC	1.65	1	—	—
CIDA	6.10	1	—	—
COFACE	0.11	1	—	—
DIGIS	0.60	1	—	—
ECOWAS Fund	2.36	1	—	—
EEC	—	—	37.06	1
EIB	39.31	2	59.35	1
Germany	—	—	9.30	1
IBRD	364.07	5	583.01	4
IDA	59.14	3	105.72	8
ISDB	8.51	2	23.01	3
IFAD	—	—	5.57	1
IFC	8.77	2	—	—
Italy	10.19	1	—	—
KFW	8.42	2	36.19	1
Kuwait Fund	8.74	1	70.28	1
Netherlands	—	—	3.67	1
Norway	3.82	2	20.76	3
ODA	—	—	4.73	1
OECF	6.43	1	—	—
OPEC Fund	8.28	2	13.69	3
SAFC	—	—	11.94	1
Saudi Fund	—	—	30.08	1
SDF	8.24	1	—	—
SIDA	5.67	1	—	—
Sweden	—	—	8.81	1
United Kingdom	—	—	30.21	1

(continued)

Table 12. (continued)

	1985		1986	
	Bank group amount	Total operations	Bank group amount	Total operations
UNSO	—	—	5.67	1
USAID	88.48	3	1.68	1
WFP	—	—	1.57	1
Bank group share	724.05	41	1,199.00	42

Note: This table does not include cofinancing among the various African Development Bank Group facilities. Cofinanciers include the following: ABEDA—Arab Bank for the Economic Development of Africa; AFESD—Arab Fund Economic Social Development; BDEAC—Banque développement États Afrique Centrale; BOAD—Banque ouest-africaine de développement (Togo); CCCE—Caisse centrale de coopération économique (France); CDC—Commonwealth Development Corporation (U.K.); CIDA—Canadian International Development Agency; COFACE—Confédération des organisations familiales de la Communauté européene (Belgium); DIGIS—Directorate General Voor International Samen Werbing (Netherlands); ECOWAS—Economic Community of West African States (Nigeria); EEC—European Economic Community; EIB—European Investment Bank; IBRD—International Bank for Reconstruction and Development (World Bank); IDA—International Development Association; ISDB—Islamic Development Bank (Saudi Arabia); IFAD—International Fund for Agricultural Development; IFC—International Finance Corporation; KFW—Kreditanstalt für Wiederaufbau (Federal Republic of Germany); ODA—Overseas Development Administration; OECF—Overseas Economic Co-operation of Japan; OPEC—Organization of Petroleum Exporting Countries; SAFC—Saudi Arabia Finance Corporation; SDF—Saudi Development Fund; SIDA—Swedish International Development Authority; UNSO—United Nations Office for the Sudano-Sahalian Region; USAID—United States Agency for International Development; WFP—World Food Programme. Source: ADB/ADF, Board of Governors. *Annual Report* (1986).

Organization (UNIDO), rehabilitation of industrial sector projects; and World Health Organization (WHO), joint project identification in primary health care. Similar cooperation agreements were concluded with Economic Commission for Africa (ECA), Organization of African Unity (OAU), the Federation of

African Consultants, PANAFTEL (Pan African Telecommunications), and Shelter-Afrique.

Interorganizational relations have expanded for two reasons. First, as economic development occurs, the number of funding opportunities expands. As basic infrastructure is developed, the demand for projects linking previous projects or maintaining projects already completed increases. Second, the international community has launched an all-out effort at improving the economic status of Africa. More IGOs, nongovernmental organizations, and bilateral donor aid agencies have targeted their allocations to African countries.

Yet as the number of organizations concerned with African economic development increases, the potential interactions among them also enhances the likelihood of political conflict (Whitaker, 1988:210). Hegemonic actors, usually donor members within other organizations, may try to impose their will, to dictate their terms and conditions for funding. Hence decisions on general issues as well as on particular projects may become more controversial. With more organizations participating as funders, there is increasing competition for scarce resources, including finance capital from the international monetary markets (bond funds), good projects, qualified personnel to manage projects and offer sound advice. For example, within the ADB, selection of a president and executive directors may depend on what countries hold similar positions in the OAU, World Bank, and International Monetary Fund (IMF). To explore conflicts occurring as a result of ADB's interactions with other organizations, a survey of interactions between the ADB and the other organizations and programs is conducted.

The International Monetary Fund was established as an institution charged with supervising international monetary arrangements. One of its major responsibilities was to provide short-term loans to finance temporary deficits. At Bretton Woods, there was discussion on whether the purposes of the loans could be better achieved through automatic or conditional lending. The IMF differentiates between two types of conditionality: low conditionality (Compensatory Financing Facility) occurs when a country acknowledges that it has a balance of payments need and announces to the IMF that it is taking measures to resolve its deficit; high conditionality occurs when the IMF requires that a country design a specific set of measures approved by the IMF to eliminate its deficit before loans are granted. (Killick, 1984:3-4; Williamson, 1982:11-12). Under high conditionality the country may be required to make both internal adjustments (following deflationary fiscal and monetary policies) and external adjustments (eliminating import controls and exchange restrictions, and devaluing its currency). Once a strategy is negotiated, the IMF monitors the adjustment programs and interprets whether performance criteria have been met. Adjustment programs may also contain policy understandings—actions that the country agrees to take, but that do not have explicit sanctions associated with nonfulfillment. "Because failure to take policy understandings seriously would also predispose the [IMF] to take an uncharitable view of any breach of the performance criteria, they are not without importance" (Williamson, 1982:36-37).

Initially most of these IMF-inspired policies were negotiated with Latin American countries; hence, much of the criticism about the IMF policies are based on the Latin American experience (Amuzegar, 1986; Honeywell, 1983; Payer, 1974).

In the 1970s the IMF became more active in Africa. The involvement intensified after the first oil crisis of the early years of the decade. Although the impact of the crisis varied by country, current account deficits of African countries averaged around 9% of GDP between 1973 and 1979, a figure much higher than in other Third World regions (World Bank, 1981a:17). Exporters of agricultural commodities experiencing price escalations could make the adjustments more easily; however, the net barter terms of trade for mineral exporters fell by an average of 7.1% following the oil crisis. Foreign reserves were depleted; debt service ratios rose from 6% in 1970 to 12.4% in 1979 (World Bank, 1981a:18). Responding to this set of conditions, the IMF's oil facility furnished 53% of the total gross flows from the IMF to Africa, serving as a cushion to the first oil shock. In addition, the IMF set up a trust fund by selling its gold holdings to provide low-cost loans to poorer member countries (Hardy, 1986:464).

It was the second oil crisis at the end of the 1970s that both devastated the economies of many African countries and solidified the IMF's expanded role in Africa. Between late 1978 and 1980 there was an 80% increase in oil prices (World Bank, 1981b). Prices of primary commodities excluding petroleum dropped; they were 13% lower in 1981 than they were in 1980. As prices fell, export volumes either declined or increased more slowly than anticipated. All this translated into serious balance of payments problems. Total deficits on the current account for sub-Saharan Africa increased by 41% in 1980 above 1979, and by another 50% in 1981 (IMF *Balance of Payments Yearbook* 1984:2, 26). The problem was widespread—deficits ranged from 3.6% of GDP in Uganda to 21% in Mauritania (World Bank, 1983: 542-43).

Thus after 1979, with the suspension of most commercial-bank lending to Africa, the IMF became virtually Africa's only source for balance of payments (non-project) financing. The average volume of IMF lending to Africa tripled. And the types of conditionality attached to the loans changed. During 1975 and 1976, low conditionality funds accounted for 80% of Africa's purchases from the IMF; after the oil crisis, higher conditionality lending increased, amounting to 75% of IMF lending to Africa (Hardy, 1986:464). In addition, medium-term adjustment programs (Extended Fund Facility [EFF] arrangements) were replaced by standby arrangements of a year to eighteen months. In mid-1986, fifteen of the thirty-one active IMF programs were in Africa (Callaghy, 1987:156). Thus, as Thomas M. Callaghy reports, "the IMF became but the leading edge of greatly increased conditionality that has now spread to almost all forms of external assistance" (1987:155).

As the IMF's role in Africa expanded, the organization has been more frequently criticized. In fact, IMF representatives even as early as 1982 were reportedly "taken aback" by the degree of hostility they encountered (Helleiner, 1983:2). The IMF has been charged with providing only a fraction of Africa's needs for balance of payments financing. For example, Chandra

S. Hardy cites figures that show decreased access to the IMF by African countries.

Africa accounts for only 3.3% of IMF quotas, and since the 1981 quota increase, access to the use of Fund resources has been reduced twice, from 150% to 95% of quotas under "normal" circumstances (115% in exceptional circumstances) and from 600% to 408% cumulatively. In net terms, sub-Saharan Africa has significantly lower access limits in 1985 than before the general quota increase. Access to the Compensatory Financing Facility has been reduced from 100% to 83% of quotas, and the practice that up to 50% of quotas was available on low conditionality terms has been withdrawn.
Net IMF credit made available to Africa between 1979 and 1983 equalled $3.7 billion, sufficient to offset only about one-quarter of the cumulative shortfall in the purchasing power of exports resulting from the 20% deterioration in the terms of trade over the period [1986:467]

The IMF has also been accused of providing funds that are too costly for Africa. Interest rates are only slightly below market and repayment periods average five years. The IMF has become one of Africa's main creditors; it was owed 50% to 75% of the debt service paid in 1984 (Hardy, 1986:467).
The IMF has also been criticized for both the content and timing of the conditionality imposed. Although most countries admit that some urgent measures are needed to ease their financial difficulties, many African leaders argue that IMF policies of demand management (such as expenditure cuts) are less appropriate than increasing the volume of exports or increasing productivity. According to the same officials, even if the policies were appropriate, reforms take time to implement. Results monitored by the IMF must be visible within one year under standby arrangements and within three to five years for other arrangements. In short, critics charge that the IMF's time horizon is too restrictive. As G.K. Helleiner elucidates, "the IMF has given inadequate consideration to these countries' limited capacity to adjust. The traditional 'blunt instruments' of IMF macroeconomic stabilization recommendations . . . all pursued within a fairly short period—cannot be expected to be as effective in the typical African country as elsewhere" (1983:19).
Last, the IMF has been accused of being unsuccessful. Even if

only a fraction of the financial needs were met and if condition-ality was acceptable, IMF stabilization programs have not been successful in Africa. IMF economists Jostin B. Zulu and Saleh M. Nsouli (1985) conclude that numerous other factors, unfore-seen developments, affect a country's implementation of adjust-ment programs. In Liberia, higher oil prices caused losses in the energy-intensive iron ore sector, contributing to a fall in tax revenues that made budgetary targets harder to meet. While Morocco was implementing its adjustment program, world de-mand for phosphate fell, leading to a shortfall in export receipts. In Senegal, economic performance was adversely affected by the Sahel drought. Similarly, IMF adjustment policies have been hampered by difficulty in mobilizing sufficient political sup-port for adjustment. Doubts about the administrative capability of the countries to implement measures necessary for adjust-ment are voiced. And in a few cases, the targets established in the program may themselves have been inadequate (Zulu and Nsouli, 1985:14, 16). The IMF just does not have the ability to influence these various factors. There have been admitted "slippages" in implementation—the emergence of unforeseen developments, delays, and shortfalls (Callaghy, 1987:157).

Despite the trenchant criticisms of the IMF, a consensus seems to have emerged among other donors, multilateral and bilateral, that economic success now depends upon the coun-try's adoption of an IMF adjustment program. Likewise, debt rescheduling is dependent on conclusion of an agreement with the IMF. Since the beginning of the 1980s, the IMF has played a constantly expanding role in Africa (see also Helleiner, ed., 1986). With this larger role, the IMF interacts more frequently with both the World Bank and ADB.

Following Bretton Woods, the IMF and World Bank collaborated very closely. The IMF's staff provided assistance to the WB and vice versa to minimize work duplication and avoid commu-nicating inconsistent advice to recipients (Hino, 1986:10-11). This collaboration was simplified by the fact that during much of the early period, at least until the 1970s, the two organiza-tions had distinct tasks. The World Bank was an institution

whose long-term loans were directed to promotion of development through project lending; and project lending appraisal and
implementation required microeconomic experts. Since the
1960s, the World Bank has limited itself to 10% for non-project
lending, with 6% more nearly the norm. These funds were
quick disbursements for countries experiencing a natural or
manmade disaster. World Bank policy dialogue rarely went
beyond "gentlemenly persuasion" (Please, 1984:24). But World
Bank projects and objectives have always had consequences for
the IMF; project loans augment long-term capital flows.

By the late 1970s, with the experience of the two oil shocks,
the World Bank concluded that acceptable rates of economic
development could not be achieved under adverse balance of
payments conditions. The bank's officials became more concerned about their inability to make effective the link between
commitment and disbursement of project-related funds and
policy issues (Please, 1984:24). So, in 1980 the World Bank introduced a new program of Structural Adjustment Lending (SAL)—
lending intended to achieve viability for medium-term balance
of payments problems, while maintaining the level and rate of
economic growth at as high a rate as possible.

Structural adjustment loans are a series of three to four dis-
crete lending operations occurring over a five- to six-year period,
providing quick disbursing balance of payments support to a
country prepared to formulate and reach agreement with the
World Bank on a program. Such a program involves financial
arrangements designed to exert discipline over level of aggregate
demand for goods and services; an external borrowing program
to monitor which goods and services would be supplemented
from abroad; and a program of structural adjustment measures
to monitor and discipline the use to which these resources are
put (Please, 1984:18-19). The structural objectives are to be
achieved within five to ten years; specified measures to be
adopted over a five-year period are delineated. In addition, the
government must agree to a monitorable set of actions before
approval or during the first-year disbursement period (Please,
1984:29). In short, under the program, the WB, in collaboration
with the borrowing country, delineates key areas in which it

judges policies to be deficient or misguided. Policy areas typically examined by WB officials under SAL include pricing policies, import liberalization measures, public investment priorities, budgetary and debt management, and balance of payments management (Girling, 1985:70). Policy reform in these areas is negotiated to correct perceived weaknesses. The World Bank's ceiling on non-project lending, however, is the one major constraint on the bank's expansion into this activity.

One of the first structural adjustment loans went to Kenya in 1980. To obtain the $55 million, the World Bank required the following measures: (1) the development of a comprehensive public investment program with full economic justification to be included in the formal budget and operations of parastatal bodies; (2) the presentation of a rationalized plan of industrial protection and a reduction in tariff levels; and (3) the implementation of a comprehensive export promotion procedure. The first requirement was met; the second, only partially, and the third, not at all. In the 1982 negotiations for an additional $61 million, the WB made it clear that the Kenyan government's failure to comply with the conditions of the loan would result in penalties. The government had to promise to continue with foreign trade liberalization and export promotion activities, and to move toward freer marketing of maize. In actuality, some implementation occurred with the first; none with the second; and only a progress report had been completed on the third (Mosley, 1986:109, 111-12). Two bilateral donors, the United States and Great Britain, even suspended negotiations on program grants until the government put the World Bank program into operation. In short, limited cross-conditionality between multilateral and bilateral donors occurred.

With the IMF's new expanded role in Africa, the organization is not only concerned with a balance of payment turnaround, but has been involved increasingly in discussing variations and policy alternatives and offering policy advice. The alteration of IMF tasks is well summarized by John Williamson:

Thus, the former distinctions between the roles of the [IMF] and the [WB]—macro versus micro, demand versus supply, adjustment versus development, financial versus real, program versus project loans, short term versus long term—have been severely eroded. . . . [T]he critical distinction now relates to the respective staffs' spheres of competence rather than to the content of their respective programs. The [IMF] staff, usually experts in macroeconomics, demand management, and payments adjustment, consult their [WB] counterparts when microeconomic supply questions like investment priorities arise, and vice versa. Both sets of expertise are regarded as valuable to the articulation of a well-conceived, medium-term adjustment program. Accordingly, in the ideal situation a country negotiates simultaneously with the [IMF] for an extended loan and with the [WB] for a SAL. When one institution alone is negotiating, it still can and should draw on the knowledge of the other to ensure an adequate overall package. Where their responsibilities overlap, their advice must be harmonized. [1982:22-23]

Although the operational tasks of the two institutions have become less distinct, some procedural differences remain. The IMF, because it traditionally dealt only with balance of payments support, usually sponsors short staff visits with counterparts in finance ministries or central banks. In contrast, the World Bank with a longer-term perspective supports missions of a longer duration. Resident representative permanently residing in many countries engage in continuous interaction with national government authorities. Despite these differences, there is regular and frequent interaction between IMF and WB economists and loan officers who work on the same countries (Hino, 1986:13).

In 1986 the World Bank and IMF collaborated formally in a new lending pool, the Structural Adjustment Facility. This lending program, comprised of $3.1 billion, is designed to aid the poorer debtor countries to revamp their economies. Eighty percent of the funds are earmarked for Africa; only the poorest recipients of International Development Association (IDA) money are eligible. Those countries are eligible to borrow as much as 47% of their quota under the IMF; 20% in the first year and 13.5% in each of the next two years. Specifically, the funds are to aid countries to develop "policy frameworks" for restructuring their economy—broad "benchmarkets" that borrowing countries must meet in restructuring their economies. Specific goals may include streamlining the tax system, reducing the role of state-run enterprises, and/or overhauling price systems. Countries that fail to meet these goals are ineligible for the second stage of their loans. Both institutions hope that monetary incentives for economic restructuring can stimulate more comprehensive reforms.

From a substantive and procedural viewpoint, what worries African countries about the increasing similarity of WB and IMF tasks and the expanded collaborative activities between the two institutions is the possibility of cross-conditionality. As WB Vice President Edward Jaycox states in *Africa Recovery* in 1987: "I know the countries are worried about us ganging up on them—cross conditionality." The World Bank has a stated policy not to be identified with cross-conditionality; assistance from one institution should not be contingent on a country's meeting the conditionality of another (World Bank *Annual Report* 1986:57). In practice, however, if a country does not meet the conditionality specified by one institution, other multilateral and bilateral support may be denied. In fact, with the increasing prominence of the IMF in Africa and with its "lead agency" status in the debt crisis, cross-conditionality is already occurring, even though informal collaboration is preferable.

Both WB and IMF officials try to obtain a consistent diagnosis of members' policies, so that policy advice can be made "consistent, complementary, and mutually reinforcing while avoiding cross-conditionality" (IMF *Annual Report* 1986:45-46). To achieve such coordination, missions to countries are jointly staffed by the two institutions. IMF and WB staff attend each other's executive board meetings, leading ideally to a broadening of the perspectives of both institutions (IMF *Annual Report* 1986:46).

ADB's relations, as suggested in chapter 7, have been most extensive with the World Bank. For most of its history, lacking funds, organizational skills, and political visibility, the ADB was clearly relegated to secondary status vis-à-vis the World Bank. Only with the adhesion of the extraregionals, the augmentation of capital, and hence increasing visibility of the institution, has that relationship begun to change. The innovations developed by the World Bank to deal with acute economic crisis, including the recognition that the WB must engage in policy dialogue and give policy advice to African governments, have been in part emulated by the ADB. And the World Bank has realized that the ADB may be an important legitimating institution for the international development community in Africa. The ADB has only reluctantly been moving in these new directions, sometimes preferring that the other institutions offer policy advice in an effort to preserve their own legitmacy.

The African Development Bank is not yet an "equal partner" with the World Bank. For example, at the Seoul meeting of the World Bank in October 1985, the Baker Plan singled out the Inter-American Development Bank (IDB) for its special role in Latin America. The initiative stated that the IDB should be encouraged to introduce major programs of well-defined economic country strategies and to support non-project lending. Nowhere in the Baker Plan was there mention of the African Development Bank playing a comparable role in Africa. In fact, the American executive director of the ADB termed this omission a "major flaw" in the initiative itself. A "trilateral approach" that included the WB, IMF, and ADB in Africa would have been more suitable. The omission, intentional or not, is symptomatic of the fact that the ADB is still not viewed as an equal to either the other regional development banks or to the World Bank.

Despite the IMF's now prominent role in Africa, direct IMF relations with the ADB are minimal. The ADB has consistently tried to distance itself from the IMF, for fear of becoming "IMFized" in the eyes of the African constituency. However, this "distance" has been increasingly difficult to maintain, especially as the international financial community ties its own aid to the establishment of IMF adjustment programs in borrowing countries. For example, in May 1987, a few days before the ADB was to consider an $18 million loan to the Zambian Development Bank, Zambia abandoned its IMF program. Faced with the dilemma of whether or not to follow the lead of other institutions which withdrew aid in the wake of Zambia's rejection of IMF policy, the ADB chose to postpone a decision "pending submission of a field report from technical staff." As the secretary general of the ADB queried, "Are you letting an African country down because it let down the IMF? " (Brooke, 1987:14). In short, the ADB has been confronted by dilemmas in trying to avoid the political pitfalls and state animosity coming from an even distant identification with the IMF.

Yet the ADB is increasingly concerned with debt issues so crucial to the IMF. In 1988 the ADB, with the assistance of a British bank, proposed a refinancing scheme that gives debtor countries a realistic payment schedule over the long term. The proposal, first revealed by President N'Diaye at the OAU summit in 1987, provides for concessional rates of interest because debtor governments have no realistic hope of repaying loans at market rates. Specifically, the scheme calls for the debts of African countries to be converted into long-term securities or bonds with a maturity of twenty years to be repaid in full. The annual level of total debt service would be negotiated. The debtor would make annual payments into a redemption fund. The rate of interest would be based on the difference between the annual payments into the redemption fund and the acceptable level of debt service negotiated. Already about fifteen governments have contacted the ADB about the possibility of implementing the plan. The major hurdle to the adoption of such a plan is the reduced rate of interest (Hodges et al., 1988:26-27). Should the ADB proposal be implemented, the organization would undoubtedly find itself in a much closer working relationship with the IMF.

As the tasks of the three institutions become less distinct, and as the level of involvement in national governments by all three institutions increases, the institutions realize that they are faced with two nagging problems. First, consistency of policy advice and uniformity of the policy dialogue toward any one country by all three institutions may be increasingly difficult to maintain. Although precise consistency may not be necessary or even desirable, especially from the perspective of the ADB, inconsistency of advice is seen by all three institutions as counterproductive. Hence, all three institutions emphasize the criticality of increased cooperation.

Among the three institutions, the IMF-ADB relationship is the weakest link. Only within the last four years has an IMF secretariat official become resident in Abidjan. Although responsibilities of that office include surveillance of the IMF program in the Ivory Coast, the IMF presence also facilitates informal coordination with the ADB. But the weak link between the ADB and IMF may be politically necessary, and therefore proper, as the American executive director at the ADB argues. Increasing African unhappiness with the IMF is illustrated by Zambia's abandoning stringent austerity measures imposed by the IMF (after lifting of cornmeal subsidies) when fierce urban violence broke out (Rule, 1987:1,4). As the ADB secretary general has stated, he does not want the Bank to become "an offshoot of the IMF and World Bank" (Brooke, 1987:14).

Second, as the three institutions (and other development organizations too) coordinate interventionist policies, the fear of direct cross-conditionality looms larger. Such cross-conditionality may be formal, if the institutions exercised a veto over a loan under consideration by the other, if the institutions agreed not to lend except with the concurrence of the other institution, or if the institution agreed jointly to interrupt access to loans. More likely, the institutions would be "guilty" of informal cross-conditionality. The institutions would independently arrive at the outcomes stated above (Dell, 1988:558-59). Avoiding both formal and informal cross-conditionality may be a political necessity if the ADB is to maintain its legitimacy. There is, however, a discrepancy between announced policy and practice over this matter. For example, in 1985 World Bank officials did approve a series of initiatives to improve aid coordination and thus avoid the difficulties discussed above. Of most relevance to coordination with the African Development Bank is the broadening of consultations from the Western Africa Regional Office of the World Bank. Part of this effort entails strengthening coordination in UNDP-sponsored roundtables, the ADB, and in the Organization for Economic Cooperation and Development (OECD) donor forums (World Bank *Annual Report* 1985:97).

ADB interactions with the other agencies within the UN system have traditionally been pro forma. Although ADB's *Annual Reports* consistently list all the cofinanced projects and/or cooperation agreements with these organizations or programs, the interaction has been rather limited. Data in table 12 substantiate the observation. In 1985 no projects were cofinanced with a UN-related agency other than the World Bank. In 1986, although 7% of projects were cofinanced with a UN-related agency, this amount represented only 2% of funds used in cofinanced projects. Both parties have been reluctant to cofinance projects for a number of reasons. The procedures employed by the development banks and by the other UN system agencies are different. Many functional UN agencies have mandates to fund only certain sectors or benefit specific constituencies. Even when projects are cofinanced, the respective UN agency provides resources for only specific portions of the project and the ADB another, with very little actual coordination between the two donors.

ADB's contacts with UN Development Program (UNDP), Food and Agriculture Organization (FAO), and International Fund for Agricultural Development (IFAD) are illustrative. The UNDP resident advisor in Abidjan circulates to the ADB copies of UNDP's country programs and country management plans (six-month time frame) for all the African countries to see if the ADB will cofinance UNDP projects. The frequency of such cofinancing is low, in part, because UNDP projects are rather small and because of the method of solicitation: each agency circulates their project pipelines in hopes of obtaining some portion of cofinancing from another institution, rather than jointly identifying projects of mutual interest. In contrast, FAO operates on a contract basis with ADB. FAO identifies projects, but does not conduct project appraisals. ADB conducts the appraisal for a fee. Among these agencies, IFAD is singled out as one of the most difficult agencies with which to coordinate. IFAD finances only food production projects aimed at the poorest groups within the population; commercially oriented food production is excluded from consideration. With this limited mandate, IFAD's possible cofinancing with ADB continues to be circumscribed.

Although these pecularities and idiosyncracies of specific UN organizations limit the amount of interorganizational relations vis-à-vis the ADB, the United Nations parent organization has singled out Africa for special treatment. This special treatment ought to provide increasing points of convergence between the ADB and the UN system agencies.

At the UN Special Session on Africa in May 1986, delegates adopted the UN Programme of Action for Africa's Economic Recovery and Development (UN-PAAERD). The document produced at the conference has rapidly become the reference point for future aid and debt relief. The program involves the following "understandings" (*Africa Recovery,* 1987; Sciolino, 1986). Governments are committed to undertake far-reaching economic reforms aimed at freeing sectors of the society from restraints that inhibit growth, especially in agriculture; governments and donor agencies are obligated to make substantial commitments to agriculture and particularly to women farmers—such measures include not only increasing the level of investment, but also assuring that producer pricing policies be remunerative; governments are committed in very broad and nonspecific terms to address issues of high fertility and mortality, as well as to incorporate different groups of the population in development planning; finally, as a concession to the donors, the governments averred that private-sector involvement should be encouraged. In return, the donors have promised more program support in priority areas, speedier disbursement, increase in concessional funds, and more coordination among donors. Full implementation of the program would require $128.1 billion between 1986 and 1990.

This document and the UN Special Session that produced it are of symbolic importance. The intense negotiations and compromises achieved between donors and borrowers were conducted in an institution where the African borrowers are more equally represented. With this consensus on the part of the international community, the African Development Bank as well as the other institutions have a more consistent mandate to target the agricultural sector and to encourage governments to pursue economic reform. Thus the United Nations Special Session ought to provide a firmer basis for interorganizational cooperation between the ADB and the UN system agencies. It is premature to evaluate whether the program enunciated actually facilitates cooperation, although the rapid implementation of the joint WB-IMF Structural Adjustment Facility suggests the strength of donor commitment.

The ADB has traditionally acknowledged its debt to its sister African international organizations, the Organization of African Unity (OAU) and the United Nations Economic Commission for Africa (ECA). At the organizational level, the three institutions try to maintain geographic balance among the major elected and appointed positions. Prominent positions in the ADB, including executive directorships, the presidency, and vice presidencies, are more likely given to individuals from countries not already represented in comparable positions in the OAU, ECA, or even from the upper leadership ranks of the World Bank or IMF. Periodically, officials from one organization intervene in disputes of another organization. The best example was OAU officials playing a key role in "l'affaire Fordwor," intervening at some critical junctures (Fordwor, 1981).

On general economic development issues, the three organizations have attempted to maintain policy consistency. As discussed in chapter 4, the Lagos Plan of Action represented a synthesis of the views of the three institutions. ADB policy on agriculture was designed to be consistent with the Lagos Plan.

Since 1985 collaboration has become institutionalized. A series of OAU conferences focused on economic rather than on the usual political/security issues. In a surprising move, the five-year program Africa's Priority Program for Economic Recovery (APPER) proposed national policy reforms to create market incentives for agricultural producers and established an institutional framework for coordinating African positions in international economic organizations ("OAU: No Distractions Please," 1985). The result was that at the UN Special Session in May 1986 the jointly coordinated officials of the OAU, ECA, and ADB played a key role and the documents produced by the group were the basis for discussion leading to the United Nations

Programme of Action for African Economic Recovery and Development 1986-90 discussed above. With that approach African countries promised to continue with major domestic economic reform and financial support from the international donor community in the amount of $46 billion was pledged ("UNPAA-ERD," *UN Chronicle*, 1986:7-18). The same institutions sponsored a subsequent conference on the same issue in Abuja, Nigeria, in June 1987.

Recent collaboration among the three organizations has focused also on the more specific issue of debt. A significant consensus on this issue, however, has never developed either among the African debtors or among the developed country creditors. The failure to generate progress on the debt issue at the UN Special Session set the tone for the discussions at Abuja, where African states considered establishing institutionalized "consultative machinery" for states to harmonize positions for presentation to the London and Paris Clubs of creditors (UN ECA 1987:14-15). Such discussions continued at the OAU summit in 1987, where ADB's President N'Diaye presented his dramatic proposal for debt repayment referred to earlier. But few African members attended; proposals were made, decisions not forthcoming.

These collaborations among the three institutions have been fraught with difficulties. First, the OAU-ADB relationship has not always been a harmonious one. For example, in 1984 the ADB was chosen to manage the Special Emergency Assistance Fund for Drought and Famine in Africa to support the OAU's relief operations. The OAU-generated funds of 2 million UA were originally publicized as a major effort by the organization to aid in drought relief. Then in 1985 the OAU called on the ADB to assist in implementing Africa's Priority Programme for Economic Recovery. In both cases, the ADB secretariat has been disappointed by the OAU's failure to deliver the funds.

Second, experts question the viability of the OAU; the organization, located in Addis Ababa, is in shambles. According to *Jeune Afrique* ("Gâchis à Addis Ababa," 1985:11-17), 77% of OAU personnel are not physically present in Addis Ababa; those that are there are unqualified for their posts. Some of the money allocated for refugee/drought relief has been found in private bank accounts of OAU officials. This flagrant example of OAU mismanagement comes on top of the confiscatory policy of the Ethiopian government toward both the OAU and the ECA. The organizations are forced to pay exceedingly high prices; living accommodations are impossible to find; and the organizations are forced to use local contractors, many of whom have gouged the organizational coffers. Given the organizational weakness of the OAU, it is not surprising that formal collaboration among the OAU, ECA, and the ADB is difficult. However, ADB's ideological invocation of OAU's continental leadership does persist, political and economic weaknesses notwithstanding.

The ADB has played more of a coordinating role for African-based subregional development organizations. For example, symposiums have been held bringing together the various development financing institutions in West Africa, including ECOWAS's (Economic Community of West African States) Cooperation, Compensation and Development Fund, the Entente Council's Mutual Aid and Loan Guaranty Fund, the West African Development Bank, and the West African Economic Community (CEAO). The purpose of such meetings is to generate funding for multilateral projects to promote regional integration (ADB, Battelle, Geneva Research Centre, 1984). However, none of these interactions has proven significant. The other organizations fill a variety of small nitches in development financing. The infrequency of interaction has lessened the probability of interorganizational cooperation and conflict.

Contrary to expectations fueled by OPEC windfalls during the oil crises in the 1980s, ADB's cofinancing with the Arab/ Islamic lending institutions have been less frequent than anticipated. Table 12 shows that in 1985, 15% of all ADB cofinanced projects were with Islamic lenders, but these projects accounted for only 5% of all funding allocated with cofinanciers. In 1986 19% of projects found Islamic cofinanciers, adding up to 11% of cofinanced expenditures. Anticipated linkages between the ADB and other Third World groups have not materialized, the Islamic agencies preferring to fund bilaterally sponsored projects in Islamic countries.

The bilateral aid agencies of the extraregional ADB member states conduct two types of programming with the ADB: project cofinancing and grants-in-aid. In table 12, cofinancing from the European and North American donors is reported. In 1985 44% of all ADB projects were cofinanced with this group, or 27% of ADB's cofinanced project funds. In 1986 both the number and amount of projects dropped to 29% of projects and 15% of funds. But the differences in planning procedures between the ADB and the respective agencies put strains on ADB's organizational skills. For example, most of the Nordic agencies like SIDA in Sweden make plans well in advance. ADB projects suitable for cofinancing come along too late for real deliberation. The Nordic agencies also tend to concentrate aid programs in a few recipient countries, whereas the ADB is obliged for political reasons to finance at least some projects in all regional states (Arnold, 1982).

Much more important from the ADB's perspective are grants-in-aid given by the bilateral agencies. These funds are usually for financing preinvestment studies (a task that the ADB cannot fund), paying the foreign exchange costs for technical assistants, or for sponsoring training programs. Most of this money is tied in broadly to what has been designated as "institution building." As more extraregional personnel are employed at the Bank on a permanent basis, bilateral funding will in all likelihood decline. These contributions represent funds above and beyond the regular contributions donated by extraregional ADB members.

Table 13 shows the total amount of bilateral (and UNDP) contributions to the ADB. Of special interest from this list is the virtual absence of France and Japan as donors through 1983. Only in 1984 did France sign the first cooperation agreement with the ADB. French reticence to contribute may be attributed to the fact that, because they were already receiving a high proportion of procurement, as illustrated in chapter 6, increased bilateral funding to obtain more procurement is unnecessary.

Most of this bilateral aid by the development agencies is tied aid. Donors insist on hiring their own nationals; preinvestment aid must be carried out by their own consultants. So donors

Table 13. Grant Funds by Bilateral and Multilateral Donors
(UA '000 and % of total received through 1985)

Sources	Amount	% Donated
Belgium	8,999	10.5
Brazil	212	.2
Canada	6,970	8.1
Denmark	3,106	3.6
Finland	259	.3
West Germany	353	.4
Netherlands	780	.9
Norway	21,957	25.6
Sweden	3,115	3.6
United States (USAID includes Landsat, Regular, and Sahel)	30,316	35.3
Switzerland	5,251	6.1
UN Development Program	4,549	5.3
Total	85,867	

Source: African Development Bank Planning and Research Department. *Compendium of Statistics* (1987).

expect to receive economic benefits. The ADB secretariat has been trying to convince donors to untie aid, so that some African consultants can participate and be trained in conducting prefeasibility studies. In response, Canada untied 20% of aid and USAID has allocated funds for hiring African nationals. In general, though, donated funds remain tied aid. Tied aid is politically vulnerable; when donors become dissatisfied or donor priorities change, this bilateral aid rapidly changes.

Table 13 shows that USAID is the largest bilateral agency donor to the ADB. Since 1968, when the first grant was given, USAID regular grants (as differentiated from the Landsat and Sahel grants described below) have totaled $28.5 million, including a 1985 grant of $15 million. Over one-half of the aid has been earmarked for financial prefeasibility studies, that is, studies of projects up to the design stage. Most of these prefeasibility studies are for industry/infrastructure projects, followed by

Table 14. USAID Grants to the African Development Bank,
1985-89

	$000	% of total
Long-term technical assistance (includes provision for ten technical assistants)	3,921	26.1%
Short-term technical assistance	1,374	9.2
Training (includes Bank staff seminars and member country seminars)		
Commodities (computerization)	495	3.3
Evaluations (midterm, final)	7,700	51.3
Preinvestment studies	6,496	43.3
Terms of reference/project evaluations	804	5.4

Source: USAID, 1985, *Project Grant Agreement between the African Development Bank and the United States of America*, AID Project No. 698-0434.

health and education, reflecting American priorities at the time. In addition, funds are earmarked for the employment of technical assistants at ADB headquarters, training institutes for the ADB secretariat and ADB member government officials, and for purchased commodities. In the latter category, most of the funds have purchased equipment for computerization of ADB operations in Abidjan. This aid has been virtually all tied aid; all the major studies are conducted by American consultants, all the training seminars led by American nationals, and all the computer equipment American-made. Out of these funds, prior to the 1985 grant, thirty-eight prefeasibility studies were completed, resulting in loans to twenty-six different countries. Ten long-term technical advisors were financed, and 281 persons participated in training seminars, 175 from the ADB itself.

In 1985 a large USAID grant to the ADB was concluded (AID Project No. 698-0434). The stated purpose of the grant is to strengthen the institutional capacity of the ADB to develop and manage projects. Table 14 reports the subject allocation of these funds. Three items are of particular interest. First, preinvestment studies are to be conducted only for agricultural or rural development projects, reflecting the new priorities of the ADB and the United States. Second, a hefty 51.3% of the total funds is allocated to evaluation. Third, all commodities purchased must be American products, and all personnel hired must be American nationals. For projects under $100,000, bids may be informally solicited, but three proposals are needed. For contracts in excess of $100,000, only American companies and personnel can compete, with USAID West Africa (REDSO/Abidjan) reviewing the top three proposals for technical qualifications.

USAID has also funded two other activities in conjunction with ADB: the purpose of the $2.8 million Special Sahel Grant (Project #625-11-995-909) was to aid the African countries in their recovery from droughts in the early 1970s. An evaluation of this grant is found in chapter 9; the Regional Onchcerciasis Area Land Satellite Related Study Grant (Landsat) is for monitoring river blindness. The initial grant in 1974 was augmented in 1977 for a total amount of $1.7 million.

This survey of interactions between ADB and development institutions other than the World Bank suggests historically an arms' length relationship. In the case of the IMF, ADB's "distance" represents calculated policy designed to maintain ADB's legitimacy across its constituency. Yet the dominance of the IMF's role in restructuring debt and certifying governmental attempts at macroeconomic policy reform continues to increase both the frequency and the intensity of IMF-ADB contacts, making ADB's struggle for autonomy more difficult in the future. Unintended cross-conditionality may be the feared result. Only ADB's relationship with USAID is as frequent, although with the exception of USAID's "tying aid" to the purchase of American commodities and personnel, USAID policy has been compatible with ADB objectives. Hence the probability of conflict between the ADB and its largest bilateral donor is reduced although the tension is currently a persistent one, as explained in chapter 10.

The lack of frequent interactions with many of the other UN development institutions, the Arab/Islamic banks, and with the small, functionally specific, subregional organizations has minimized any conflict (or cooperation) with the ADB. Even when projects are cofinanced, differences in procedures tend to segment the project among cofinancing institutions. In contrast, ADB's relationship with the other African international organizations has become stronger, but not in project cofinancing, the traditional mode of interaction. The OAU, ECA, and ADB have increasingly sought to coordinate not just administrative policies, but also substantive policies and approaches to economic development strategy. Institutionalized collaboration is frequent, although major obstacles impede the process.

The ADB's Evaluation Process

All of the multilateral development banks including the African Development Bank have instituted formal procedures of evaluation. These evaluations are designed to serve multiple purposes. At minimum, they assess the efficiency of internal decision-making procedures—whether the different units, including the president, secretariat personnel, and executive directors, performed according to the technical prerequisites of a functional organization. They ought to evaluate the performance of recipient governments in conducting the project, including both private contractors and state overseers. At maximum, such project evaluations ought to include an assessment of relative success: Did the project actually achieve economic expectations? Did economic benefits outweigh costs? Did the project contribute to the state's economic development? Competent project evaluators should be able to discover points in the project cycle where political factors overrode technical considerations, where economic shortcomings can be attributed to political failures, and where economic impact may have political salience. From an analysis of ADB evaluations we confirm our expectation that multilateral development banks are political institutions.

The United States has played a key role in pushing the multilateral development banks toward evaluation. In 1968 the Selden Amendment directed the American executive director in the Inter-American Development Bank to seek the establishment of an independent evaluation unit for post-project review. This initiative broke IDB inertia and the evaluation unit was established. The group is independent of the IDB staff and directly responsible to the executive directors (U.S. Senate Committee on Foreign Relations, 1977:11).

In 1973 American legislation authorized the American executive director in the World Bank to support comparable procedures. As a result, the IBRD Operations Evaluation Department, consisting of professional analysts and consultants, con-. ducts evaluations. Bank management then submits the evaluation reports to the executive directors for review and comment. However, the IBRD and IDB evaluations emphasize different dimensions: IDB officials assess internal management capability; the IBRD, contributions the projects make to economic development (U.S. Congressional Research Service, 1974: 85-87). Both dimensions of the evaluations are of interest to the United States as the largest financial contributor to each institution (U.S. Department of the Treasury, 1982).

The World Bank approach to evaluation has become the guide for numerous development agencies, the model to be emulated should financial resources be available. Because of its importance as a model, the approach is described in some detail (Baum and Tolbert, 1985:383-85). Two years after completion of disbursements, every WB-assisted project is reviewed by operational staff who prepare a project completion report. When possible, this report is completed by those who were directly involved in preparation and implementation of the project. About half of these projects are selected for a detailed performance audit by staff from the Operations Evaluation Department, an independent group reporting directly to the executive directors. Approximately 10% of these projects are selected at random, the others are chosen to delineate various sector and country comparisons. This assessment is conducted by reading files, interviewing staff, and visiting project sites. Evaluation is based on the net present value of the project, the internal rate of return, the cost-benefit ratio, and a sensitivity analysis designed to show how sensitive the net present value (or internal rate of return) is to variations in selected costs and benefits. The World Bank publishes an *Annual Review of Project Performance Audit Results*, which summarizes the various indicators. Finally, for a select group of projects, the unit conducts an impact evaluation five years or more after project completion. The longer-term assessment addresses the question of whether the project has had not only its expected economic impact, but its institutional and social impact as well. Hence in the model World Bank process, both post hoc evaluations and longer-term impact assessments comprise evaluation.

The African Development Bank initiated evaluation procedures in 1977; in 1980 an evaluation division was formally created in the Planning and Research Department. Both the World Bank model outlined above and the experience of ADB's participation with the U.S. Agency for International Development in the extensive evaluation of USAID's Sahel grants program stimulated the ADB to institute evaluation procedures.

The joint ADB/USAID (1980) report assessed the efficacy with which the ADB utilized USAID bilateral technical assistance funds for preinvestment studies of specific projects. The study concluded that utilization of funds was delayed because of inadequate preinvestment studies leading to contractor bottlenecks. Specifically, ADB was singled out for shortcomings in its implementation of the projects. Problems with consultants selected and monitored by ADB were particularly detrimental. For example, some projects like the Swaziland Mahamba-Manzini Road and the Mali Markala-Niono Road were overdesigned and inappropriate to conditions in the country; North American standards of width and clearances were utilized. Some of the consultants were technically incompetent (Zaire, Kwango, Wanba, Bombo, and Lufimi River bridges); proper geological assessment of the soil did not precede boorings. Other projects showed lack of social sensitivity, for example, constructing transportation arteries on sacred grounds (Senegal, the Ziguinchor-Cap Skirring Road). The ADB was not the only weak institution. The national government authorities were also at fault for not being cognizant of their various responsibilities in overseeing the project. The USAID evaluation reads like a litany of errors in development financing (ADB/USAID, 1980).

As a result of the joint ADB/USAID evaluation, ADB officials realized that their own performance was seriously deficient; administrative inefficiency adversely affected the achievement of goals. ADB officials participating in the evaluation also recognized the importance donors give to evaluation. Hence, the establishment of institutionalized evaluation procedures became all the more imperative. Even after ADB's implementation of evaluation procedures, the 1985 USAID grant to ADB discussed in chapter 8 allocated 51.3% of funds for evaluation studies, a confirmation of the importance that donor attaches to evaluation.

According to the terms of reference of the evaluation unit within the ADB (ADB Planning and Research Department, 1981), its responsibility is to examine completed projects to determine whether or not the intended benefits to a given economy are being realized and to assess the project's impact on member states' economic and social development. The ultimate purpose is to learn lessons from the experience. To achieve these objectives, the evaluators compare original targets at appraisal and actual results, analyze the factors that contributed to success or failure of projects, and examine the impact on the national economy. Several types of evaluation are conducted: post hoc evaluations of single completed projects, sectoral analyses, country or regional evaluations, and impact evaluations for longer-term assessments, as well as ongoing evaluations to adjust objectives and redesign projects during the implementation phrase.

For several reasons, however, evaluation procedures have been slow to develop in the ADB. First, only 200 projects have been completed by the ADB, as evidenced by the submission of the Project Completion Reports. The total number of candidates for project evaluation is relatively small. Although these reports are due six months after completion of the projects, many are late, delaying the two-year hiatus between project completion and evaluation. With few projects evaluated, intercountry and intersectoral comparisons are problematic. Second, the post hoc evaluation unit has generally employed about eight evaluators. For on-site evaluation visits, either one person is sent for three weeks or two persons for two-week visits. Thus the unit is able to conclude only about twenty post hoc evaluations a year—a small subset of the projects completed. Third, there remains a lack of systemization and completeness in the evaluation process. Projects and sectors are only evaluated according to economic criteria: Has the project achieved the economic goals stipulated in the appraisal report? Socioeconomic analysis is characteristically absent, despite the acknowledged utility of such information. What is actually being evaluated is how well Bank officials performed in estimating economic rates of return in the project appraisal report. Although such information is useful in evaluating appraiser's competence, it is less useful for analyzing the contribution of the specific project to a country's economic and political development.

Because the post-evaluation reports reflect the performance of the Bank's personnel, they are often ignored; even summary evaluation reports are not widely read. For psychological and pragmatic reasons, daily considerations prevail. The results of post hoc evaluation reports have only slowly been disseminated in the organization. And ADB contractors and consultants being evaluated in the reports do not even receive a copy. Poor reception of the reports has also dampened the enthusiasm of many executive directors for post hoc evaluation. Such limitations defeat the longer-term objective of post hoc evaluation—to implement better projects and policies.

Generalizations concerning ADB's performance on projects have never been published. Even the sectoral assessments that are designed to collate the findings of various projects in different countries have not included intersectoral comparisons. Nevertheless, interview data and scrutiny of evaluation reports yield some tentative generalizations.

ADB projects evaluated as most successful according to economic rates of return have been road projects. Such projects are relatively easy to carry out and their economic evaluation is straightforward, although the two years' time lapse between project completion and evaluation may be too short to analyze permanent changes in transportation networks. For example, one African Development Fund project evaluated most highly by Bank officials is the John Mzumara-Ekuendeni Road in Malawi, a thirty-two kilometer stretch of road serving as a north to south link in the country (ADB, Evaluation Division, 1984). The internal rate of economic return on the project was 7.25%. The selected contractor for the road had completed a road nearby; hence materials were well positioned and the project started quickly. Consultants on the project were experienced. The Malawian government satisfied all preconditions rapidly and the governmental executing agency was well organized and well managed. The road was still in excellent condition three years later, with traffic beginning to approach the optimistic projections predicted in the appraisal report. Ironically, the worst performer on the project from a procedural viewpoint was the African Development Fund. Fund officials failed to track adequately disbursements; they were slow to disburse and had instituted no procedure to confirm immediate payment. Yet the single project was deemed economically successful.

Transportation projects are not uniformly successful. For example, in the Banjul (Gambia) Yundum International Airport project (ADB, Planning and Research Department, 1985), project appraisers widely overestimated expected increases in tourist traffic due to the airport expansion. Two years after completion, the number of planes landing declined, although the number of passengers deplaning increased. Actual cost of the project was 110% of appraisal, but some components had cost overruns much higher. And the project's anticipated economic spin-offs from increased tourism, including earning more foreign exchange and reviving the handicraft sector, never materialized. The result was that the economic rate of return for the project was 4% (deflated figure), compared to the 9% assumed at the time of appraisal. So although transportation projects have enjoyed relative success, the record is not unblemished. In neither case was the project's contribution to the state's economic development objectives analyzed.

In contrast, agriculture, water, and national development bank projects have been among the least successful for the ADB. In fact prior to the reemphasis on food crops in the mid-1980s, agricultural projects had the worst record. Such projects depend on the cooperation of the largest number of people, are most sensitive to the precise timing of inputs, and most susceptible to climatic variabilities. The unsatisfactory evaluation of so many water projects is attributed to a different problem. Tracing the economic benefits of water projects has proven to be an elusive task, because beneficiaries are so dispersed and the benefits such as better health and higher agricultural productivity are subject to time lags greater than the two-year evaluation period. Finally, loans to national development banks are not successful, failing in too many cases to funnel money to smaller borrowers.

A few examples drawn from ADB's evaluations confirm these generalities and illustrate the reasons for the problems encountered in these sectors. Agriculture and water (irrigation) projects are often linked. In a 1972 irrigation scheme in Somalia, Afgoi-Mordile project (ADB, Evaluation Division, 1984), agricultural land was to be developed for the production of sesame, seed cotton, groundnuts, and maize. Land was to be cleared and levelled, an irrigation system installed, and power infrastructure provided. But the evaluation report shows that one year after target completion, only 50% of the land had been developed and cost overruns were already 46% of appraisal cost estimates. Although one half of the land was eventually cultivated, four years later less than 13% remained under cultivation. Another project in Tunisia, Medjerda Lower Valley (ADB, Evaluation Division, 1984), aimed at resettling farm families on newly irrigated land. The project objectives were not achieved because of inadequate extension services, rigid price policy, and a legally ambiguous land tenure system—all governmental policies that the ADB did not try to change.

The loans to national development banks are designed to channel money for small projects implemented by small- or medium-sized enterprises. One post-evaluation report of loans to the Kenyan and Tanzanian national development banks (ADB, Planning and Research Department, 1982) found procedural inadequacies that made achievement of these goals unlikely. Although the general conditions and terms under which the ADB makes such loans are reasonable, the specific criteria for disbursement has never been made explicit, and hence they are subject to diverse interpretations. Many of the loans from the two national development banks actually went to non-nationals, usually politically connected individuals managing medium or large concerns located in urban areas. Many of the enterprises required imported materials, making profitability dependent on external variabilities. For example, the success of one Kenyan project (Wirke Products) depended on having the foreign exchange necessary to purchase imported machinery. In a Tanzanian twine and rope works, whose outputs were largely destined for export, a worldwide recession resulted in a decline to 25% of plant capacity. In the same country a loan to a fishnet manufacturer required importation of 85% of the primary products. Getting the currency necessary to finance the inputs became a constant source of difficulty and underutilization of capacity a perennial problem. Once the funds are committed to these projects, the ability of ADB (or other bilateral and multilateral financiers) to monitor projects diminishes substantially. When ADB lost its ability to enforce criteria for disbursal as it did for the national development bank loans, the organization could no longer monitor projects. Such projects show consistently low rates of return.

The ADB has conducted very few sector analyses because of both personnel limitations and methodological shortcomings. Sectoral experts, already in short supply, are needed for the evaluation. If utilized, current projects requiring sectoral experts are delayed. To be methodologically sound, the projects should have been completed around the same time period; this limits severely the number of possible candidates. And methods of aggregating findings from different projects are inadequate, thus weakening the power of generalization based on statistical techniques.

A 1984 evaluation report did examine seven electricity projects in Africa in addition to a documentary review of an unspecified number of other electricity projects. It was found that although ADB's disbursement performance was satisfactory, project implementation was poor. In one case two gas turbines had been installed, instead of four; in another, instead of four transformer stations and four transmission lines, five transformer stations were completed. In both cases, the Bank was not even aware of these major modifications, a clear indication of lapses in project monitoring and supervision. Such failures can also be attributed to the fact that preinvestment studies are rarely financed for the sector. Ironically, this sectoral evaluation did not compare economic rates of return or any other economic indicators of long-term impact. The evaluation was confined to ADB performance during the appraisal and implementation phase. In light of these shortcomings, no generalizations concerning the contribution of the electricity sector to economic development can be offered.

ADB's movement into non-project lending has never been formally evaluated post hoc by the institution. Because this aid involves general budgetary support to foster specific reforms, blending into foreign exchange holdings, it is all the more difficult to evaluate. Thus little is known about effectiveness of the overall approach (Berg, 1986:515). The difficulty of evaluating the effectiveness of such funding is one reason the multilateral donors have refrained from such loans until the economic vicissitudes of the 1970s demanded new avenues of multilateral financing.

The World Bank, however, has tried to conduct assessment of non-project lending in South Asia. That study found that countries receiving substantial non-project aid performed more successfully than nonrecipient countries. But the final verdict for non-project lending remains unclear (Berg, 1986:516), as the number of confounding economic, social, and political variables unrelated to the WB's funding multiplies. The ADB has not yet attempted such an analysis. It is unlikely to do so given resource and personnel constraints at headquarters and the still relatively small proportion of ADB funds channeled into non-project lending.

Forced into posthoc evaluation by both pressure from extra-regional donors to the African Development Fund and by its technical assistance contracts with USAID, the ADB established evaluation machinery comparable in structures and purposes to the other multilateral development banks. But contrary to stated aspirations, post hoc evaluation of a few projects two years after completion remains ADB's *modus operandi*. The criteria for the evaluation remains narrowly economic and longer-term impact assessments largely absent.

Generalizations on the subtantive findings of these evaluations have not yet been attempted. Waning enthusiasm by the executive directors for making post hoc evaluation more comprehensive and more generalizable may be one explanation. Another may well be the difficulty of evaluating the relative effectiveness of a single project or even a sector in light of the multitude of uncontrollable variabilities in so many African economies during the 1970s and 1980s. However, the findings of the World Bank, with respect to its projects in Africa, may stimulate the ADB to expand post hoc evaluation to enhance its opportunity for more funding. The World Bank found that its "projects in Africa do not perform as well as projects in more robust economies. [But] aided projects generally do succeed in Africa—although not by as large a margin in other parts of the world" (Berg, 1986:518). ADB's projects do achieve some of their announced objectives. How the ADB as a political institution compares with the other multilateral development banks is examined in chapter 10.

Politics in the Multilateral Development Banks

In the first nine chapters, the African Development Bank is viewed as a political institution in three arenas—relations within the ADB, interorganizational relations, and to a lesser extent relations of the ADB with the hegemons. A revealing finding is that even with the adhesion of the extraregionals, hegemonic influence has been relatively muted. In this chapter, using the same categories of analysis, the World Bank, Inter-American Development Bank, and the Asian Development Bank are compared in view of our assessment of the ADB. Table 15 presents basic data about these respective institutions. We begin by examining the arena that is the least subject to controversy in the ADB, the hegemonic actor. According to most of the literature on the multilateral development banks, the hegemon is responsible for most political controversy.

Hegemonic Politics

The most frequent explanation for the failure of functionalism and disenchantment with economic neutrality in international economic organizations rests with the power and instrumentalities exercised by hegemonic actors. In the post–World War II international organizations, the Big Powers expected IGO policies and outcomes to be compatible with their national interests. In the multilateral development banks the economic hegemons have three avenues of influence. First, because a state's monetary contribution determines its share of votes, hegemons

Table 15. The Multilateral Development Banks Compared: Basic Characteristics, 1985 (US $ billion)

	Asian Development Bank	World Bank	Inter-American Development Bank	African Development Bank
Founding date	1966	1945	1959	1964
Established headquarters	Manila	Washington, D.C.	Washington, D.C.	Abidjan
Assets	9.0	76.0	14.3	2.4
Borrowings	5.5	50.2	9.3	1.1
Paid-in capital	1.9	5.1	2.3	1.5
Callable capital	14.0	53.7	24.4	4.4
Profitability (%)	8.0	7.6	7.5	6.3
Liquidity (%)	78.7	68.8	43.5	44.5
Loans outstanding	4.5	41.4	8.6	1.1
Loans approved 1985	1.9	11.4	2.8	1.3

Profitability = Income Before Interest as a proportion of Total Assets; Liquidity = Liquid Assets—cash plus investments—as a proportion of Undisbursed Loans

Note: Loans exclude ADF, IDA, Special Funds, special section, or other concessional lending. Source: Japan Credit Rating Agency, Tokyo, as reprinted in Wilson (1987:348).

seek a distribution of shares and votes that guarantee their influence. Second, hegemons try to influence specific policies of the banks that are not subject to direct voting. Third, they utilize a variety of financial tactics (including threats to withhold replenishments and payment arrears) to reinforce state positions on both questions of specific loans to countries (or group of countries) and on specific policies. In the event of the incompatability between organizational policies and the national interest of the hegemon, the hegemon is prepared to use its full complement of instruments to achieve its objectives. By bargaining over distribution of votes, supporting one policy approach over any others, and by manipulating financial instrumentalities, the hegemon exerts influence within the multilateral development banks, thereby undermining technical neutrality.

All of the multilateral development banks depend financially on subscription shares purchased by national governments and on selling shares in the private international capital markets of the United States, Western Europe, and Japan. Table 16 reports the subscription shares and contributions held by the four largest contributors to each of the multilateral development banks, as well as the voting power that each of these subscribers wields.

Table 16 shows unequivocally that economic dominance as represented in contributions does not directly translate into political power exercised through voting. "Voluntary" contributions to special funds, not considered part of ordinary contributions, are not included in calculating weighted voting shares. Thus, in many cases, including the World Bank group, the voting power of the major donors such as the United States and Japan is underrepresented when total subscriptions and supplementary resources are aggregated. The same is true in the African Development Fund, the Inter-American Development Bank, and the Asian Development Bank. In no case does the major donor possess more voting power under the weighted voting system than its contributions warrant.

Although voting power is not necessarily proportionate to contributions, voting power does guarantee hegemonic influence for certain types of decisions. For example, in the Inter-American Development Bank, most types of decisions, including regular loans, require only a majority vote. But two types of decisions require a majority of both Latin and North American votes. Decisions on loans made from the Fund for Special Operation and decisions on increasing capitalization, expanding the number of executive directors, and suspension from membership, each require approval of two-thirds of the countries holding three-quarters of the voting power. Hence the United States, the hegemonic power in that institution, has a blocking veto.

A procedure that can both strengthen and undermine the power of the largest contributors to the multilateral develop-

Table 16. The Multilateral Development Banks Compared: Subscriptions and Voting Power of the Four Largest Donors (% of total)

World Bank Group			*IBRD*	
	Total subscriptions and supplementary resources	Voting power	Subscription to capital stock	Voting power
United States	29.95	18.61	20.98	19.88
Japan	17.75	8.35	6.20	5.90
Fed. Rep. of Germany	11.63	7.01	5.22	4.97
United Kingdom	9.11	6.45	5.92	5.63

Inter-American Development Bank

	Suscriptions-ordinary capital and interregional capital	Voting power	Fund for Special Operations	Total subscriptions and FSO funds
United States	35	34.51	55	39
Argentina	12	11.61	6	10
Brazil	12	11.61	6	11
Mexico	7	7.46	4	7

African Development Bank/African Development Fund

	Bank-ordinary capital resources	Bank voting power	Fund subscriptions		Fund voting power
Nigeria	9.94	9.28	U.S.	13.96	6.54
Egypt	5.73	5.78	Jap.	13.68	7.09
United States	5.61	5.51	Can.	9.39	5.61
Japan	4.62	4.68	Fed. Rep.	9.03	4.45

Asian Development Bank/Asian Development Fund

	Ordinary bank capital	Voting power	Fund contributions
Japan	12.5	12.53	37
United States	12.5	12.36	—
India	—	6.05	—
Australia	—	5.57	—

Sources: World Bank *Annual Report* (1986); Inter-American Development Bank *Annual Report* (1986); African Development Bank *Annual Report* (1986); Wilson (1987).

ment banks is consensus decision making. Although consensus is employed in all the institutions, the Asian Development Bank has utilized the technique most successfully to Japan's advantage. Japan's "unspoken" implicit power means that actual votes need not be cast. The Japanese executive director often remains silent during meetings, preferring to stay aloof from discussions, but the Japanese position is known, disseminated through informal channels (Yasutomo, 1983:179). So even when hegemons may not have their "full share" of votes compared to contributions, they may prefer the consensus approach and utilize it to effective advantage.

Nevertheless, donors fight over relative voting shares. The examples of the United States in the Inter-American Development Bank, Japan in the International Development Association, and Japan in the Asian Development Bank illustrate the recent tendency of hegemons to fight for what they perceive as a "fair share" in terms of voting power.

In 1986 the United States proposed basic changes in the IDB voting procedures to guarantee greater voting control in the organization. Most loans are routinely approved by votes of more than 50%. The United States proposed that 65% of votes be required to pass loans. With 34.5% of the votes, the United States could effectively block loans ("IADB Approves Borrowing by Chile as U.S. Abstains," 1986:102-3). The proposal was controversial for two reasons. First, in the Latin view, such a proposal represented an attempt by the Americans to assert traditional creditor dominance over the institution. Second, the proposal, along with other suggestions for policy changes discussed below, was linked explicitly to American replenishment of bank funds. In the words of U.S. Department of Treasury official James Conrow, "We cannot agree to a replenishment without the necessary reforms" (Friedland, 1987:2).

The United States stood alone in these demands for changes in voting, other donors opposing the American veto demand. Only Canada appeared "lukewarm" about the proposal (Pine, 1987b:8). The decision concerning the voting change was therefore postponed several times. Finally, in April 1987, when Brazil, Mexico, Argentina, and Venezuela reiterated their opposition,

the United States announced that it would withdraw the proposal and scrap plans for a replenishment amounting to $20
billion over the next four years (Pine, 1987a). The hegemon's
attempt to assume an even greater voting share in the organization failed, but the economic cost of the decision for the IDB
appears substantial.

Political controversy also erupted over voting shares as a
percentage of contributions in the International Development
Association, the soft-loan facility of the World Bank. Japan has
sought to increase its share of voting in both institutions. In
1984 Japan was given 4.99% voting rights in the World Bank,
compared to 20.1% for the United States and 4.97% for the
Federal Republic of Germany. Japan has argued that this figure
does not adequately reflect its economic prowess, which is two
times greater than that of the Federal Republic. More important,
the voting share is far less than Japan's proportionate share of
contributions to IDA. In the seventh replenishment of IDA,
American voting power was 20.10%, whereas its slice of IDA
contributions was 25.0%. Japan had 4.99% voting shares, even
though its contributions were 18.7% of the total. In contrast, the
Federal Republic had 4.97% voting shares, although its contributions were only 11.5% of the replenishment. This discrepancy
between contributions and voting rights remains a highly controversial issue for Japan.

In the Asian Development Bank, the Japanese have expressed
dissatisfaction with the fact that voting shares are determined
by ordinary shares subscribed. Japan's voting power is relatively
equal to that of the United States even though Japan contributes
more through the Asian Development Fund. The Japanese representative has argued that the government needs domestic
public support for the bank. To muster public support, "The
current discrepancy between our shares in the Asian Development Fund and ordinary capital resources is still too large and
must be alleviated" (quoted in Wilson, 1987:135.) The American
position has been that Asian Development Fund contributions
are voluntary and have no legal or moral bearing on voting rights
in the bank, a position that the United States alone supports. To

justify the claim that the United States should maintain parity
with Japan in votes, the Americans insist that the bank consider
overall American contributions to Asia through channels other
than the development bank. Credit should be given for the
American defense umbrella over the region and how the huge
American trade deficit with the region contributes to the economic development of specific countries (Hye, 1988:28).

The controversy between the two largest donors concerns
overall political influence. As Victor H. Frank, the American
executive director to the bank in 1988, stated, "U.S. influence
on the bank isn't as strong as it should be. It is the Japanese who
run the bank" (quoted in Hye, 1988:28). He further asserts that
Japan's donations to the Asian Development Fund are helping to
boost its influence in Asia. "I don't know if we're getting less
influence, they're just getting more influence" (quoted in Hunt,
1988:10). Although redistribution of votes is not on the immediate agenda, the jockeying for hegemonic influence is likely to
continue. As one of the bank's three vice presidents, a German,
aptly summarizes, "The one who has the money calls the tunes.
That's what the U.S. did in the past and now others want their
turn" (quoted in Hunt, 1988:10). This controversy may become
more intense if the Soviets apply for membership, as anticipated
in the late 1980s. Soviet membership would fuel the contention
that the bank is taking a turn to the left since the People's
Republic of China joined in 1986 (Rosett, 1988:17). Soviet membership would necessarily lead to further redistribution of votes,
highlighting the tension already present.

Hegemonic actors like the United States and Japan are willing to use political capital to muster an increasing share of
voting power. The relative lack of American hegemonic power
in the African Development Bank is easily explained by the low
level of contributions and hence voting power. In the words of
Donald Sherk, American executive director to the ADB: "Perhaps the next most important difference was the relative
strength of our subscriptions in the other MDBs—as contrasted
with the smaller 5.6% in the African Bank" (quoted in U.S.
House of Representatives, 1986:173). But when there is no or-

ganizational provision for hegemonic influence, hegemons may turn to alternative channels.

Hegemons or would-be hegemons do use other techniques of influence. The hegemons in all the multilateral development banks use their power to both promote specific policies compatible with their national interests or to prevent passage of policies deemed incompatible with or inimical to their interests, just as the extraregional donors have tried in the African Development Bank.

The United States as the hegemon in the World Bank and Inter-American Development Bank has pressured the banks to develop lending programs compatible with American priorities. In some cases, the United States has supported economic development preferences and stated them explicitly in the legislation concerning the multilateral development banks. In other cases, the Americans have tied funding to support of certain policies.

One of the most important programmatic thrusts encouraged by the United States during the 1970s was "growth with equity." Two amendments to the Foreign Assistance Act of 1961 spell out this new interest in development programming.

U.S. policy in both bilateral and multilateral aid is to emphasize support for countries pursuing development strategies designed to meet basic human needs and self-sustaining growth with equity. [sec. 102]

U.S. participation in the multilateral banks is to place appropriate emphasis on the principle that development aid should help the poor majority in recipient countries participate in equitable growth and also participate increasingly in decisions which affect their lives. [Sec. 102, quoted in Sanford, 1982:193]

This programmatic thrust had an immediate impact in the World Bank because its president, Robert McNamara, was already advocating a poverty orientation. Immediately, higher priority was given complex, integrated rural projects with social services, like water supplies and health care (Ayres, 1983). In this case, there appears to have been a symbiosis, with World Bank and American government officials reaching independently a consensus for a poverty approach to development at about the same time (Ascher, 1990).

In 1981 the Inter-American Development Bank announced a similar policy change, commiting on paper 50% of lending to the poorest people (U.S. Senate, 1981), in contrast to between 8% and 20% traditionally targeted for such loans. There is no clear evidence, however, that such a shift in spending priorities actually occurred. During the mid-1980s the productive sectors (agriculture, industry, mining, tourism) and physical infrastructure (energy, transportation, communications) still accounted for over 80% of all loans, whereas social infrastructure and urban development loans directly benefiting the poor amounted to only 16% of lending. This seems to be a well-established pattern beginning as early as 1965 with the formation of the Fund for Special Operations (FSO) (DeWitt, 1987:277). FSO, largely financed by American contributions, tied project purchases to American exports. For borrowing governments, it became economically attractive to propose projects with higher import content (such as infrastructure), rather than for social projects requiring higher local contributions (DeWitt, 1987: 280). Thus the IDB is an excellent example of an institution in which the United States was able to forge the direction of specific policies early in the bank's history. When the American government purportedly changed its programmatic priorities in the 1970s, the Inter-American Development Bank never did alter its sectoral lending patterns, the rhetoric notwithstanding.

The United States has never had as great an impact on sectoral lending priorities in the Asian Development Bank. In that bank, a significant portion of lending has gone to infrastructure (38.2%) or directly productive activities (agriculture and industry, 34.2%). In 1986 only 13.6% of loans were destined for poverty-related projects, water supply and sanitation, urban, education, health, and population projects (Asian Development Bank *Annual Report* 1986).

One of the most important programmatic thrusts of the mid-1980s has been the American-stimulated support for privatization. Privatization has had a strong impact on the thinking and operations of all the multilateral development banks. The United States has had the most difficulty convincing officials of the Asian Development Bank about the necessity of

privatization. Although the bank did make a public commitment to "equity operations" unsecured by government guarantees, the fact is that private sector projects have been few. And
while the United States was pleased to support the Asian Development Bank's conference on privatization, bank members disagree openly about the utility of privatization. Officials themselves have stated that they are trying to distinguish between
"the ideology" of privatization (where the bank should not take
a position) and questions of economics "where privatization
may be useful" (Rafferty, 1985:187-88). The Japanese, in contrast, have taken a much more pragmatic stance on privatization. As one financial power in the organization, this position
has best served Japanese interests, whereas the United States
may have isolated itself by its stridency on this issue.

The general thrust of American-supported development programs has influenced World Bank and Inter-American Development Bank thinking, but American influence has not been as
successful with respect to specific loan provisions imposed by
the U.S. Congress on the multilateral development banks. For
example, in 1974, the Percy Amendment stipulated that integration of women into MDB programs was a high priority. Although some attention was given the status of professional
women in the banks themselves, little was done for over a
decade to encourage programs affecting the conditions and status of women in the less-developed countries. The African Development Bank has rhetorically supported the goal and it along
with the other banks now has an officer responsible for integrating the concerns of women in bank projects. The 1976 Long
Amendment advocating the use of intermediate capital and
appropriate technology elicited a positive response from the
Inter-American Development Bank. The board of executive directors accepted this provision rapidly and both the Asian Development Bank and the African Development Bank have
moved in a similar direction.

Another technique of hegemonic influence on policies in the
MDBs has involved limiting loans to countries whose regimes
are politically unacceptable to the hegemon. Most commen-
tators see such political targeting as having the most potential

to jeopardize the bank's economically neutral position. In the case of the United States, the Congress has attached amendments to appropriations which stipulate that the American executive directors in the multilateral development banks vote against loans to countries with regimes deemed unacceptable to the United States. The most important of these amendments include the Gonzalez Amendment of 1972 requiring the American representatives to oppose loans to countries that expropriate American investments; the Long Amendment (1974) requiring American representatives to oppose World Bank concessional loans (IDA) for countries that, after exploding a nuclear device, fail to sign the nuclear nonproliferation treaty; and the Harkin Amendment (1976) requiring that American representatives to the IDB and African Development Fund vote against loans for countries that consistently engage in gross violations of internationally recognized human rights, unless the loan would explicitly benefit poor people of the borrower country. Although the American president has often signed such guidelines into law, the initiatives appear to have originated in Congress, often without the support of the executive branch (U.S. Senate, 1977:5-7).

American policymakers have not been uniformly effective in imposing restrictions on loans to certain groups of countries. In some cases, executive displeasure with the amendment allowed authorities to skirt the legislative mandate. In other cases, American executive directors in the banks simply made little effort to persuade other executive directors to vote in the same direction. Sometimes American compliance has been very strong; for example, American executive directors in the banks have consistently opposed loans to countries that expropriate American investments without adequate compensation. The World Bank generally has not proceeded with these loans. Although officials in the Inter-American Development Bank have argued that multilateral loans should not be linked with bilateral investment disputes, they, too, have exercised caution, in obvious deference to the American position.

The Harkin Amendment was reinforced under Section 701 of the International Financial Institutions Act (1980). The act mandates that a quarterly human rights report be presented on countries seeking MDB loans. It also requires American executive directors at each bank to use "voice and vote" to channel assistance toward countries other than those whose governments engage in a "consistent pattern of gross violations of internationally recognized human rights."

Table 17 shows that the United States has frequently opposed loans for human rights violations in borrowers from both the Inter-American Development Bank and the Asian Development Bank. In contrast, American use of the veto was infrequent in the African Development Fund, although in the mid-1980s the United States opposed loans to Ethiopia on the basis of expropriation of American property without adequate compensation, not on the equally applicable human rights justification. Under the Reagan administration the human rights orientation has diminished support. Nevertheless, the U.S. House of Representatives still reiterates,

The consistent and apolitical enforcement of the human rights provisions applicable to U.S. votes in the multilateral development banks is of great importance to the Committee.

The Committee reminds the officials charged with carrying out the requirements of this law that it believes that vigorous enforcement of the human rights requirements adhering to U.S. participation in the multilateral development banks is critical to the maintenance of working majorities in the Congress willing to support funding of these institutions. Any perception that enforcement of this law is uneven, lax or politicized threatens to alienate precisely those members of Congress who have traditionally provided consistent support for these institutions and cannot be afforded in the present legislative climate. [1983]

The United States has continued to oppose loans to specific regimes incompatible with its interests. Nicaragua represents an instructive case of the insertion of political criteria into the lending process. Since 1982 the United States has successfully stalled a $59.8 million loan for a Nicaraguan farm project in the Inter-American Development Bank. By 1984, other countries began complaining about American blocking action (Bird and Holland, 1985:231). Secretary of State George Shultz argued

Table 17. U.S. No Votes and Abstentions on MDB Loans for
Human Rights, 1977-80

Institution	Number of times	Countries affected
IBRD	18	Argentina, Chile, El Salvador, Guatemala, Paraguay, Philippines, Uruguay
IDA	17	Afghanistan, Benin, Ethiopia, Laos, Yemen
IFC	12	Argentina, South Korea, Philippines, Uruguay
Asian Development Bank	21	Afghanistan, South Korea, Laos, Philippines, Vietnam
Inter-American Development Bank	25	Argentina, Chile, El Salvador, Guatemala, Paraguay, Uruguay
African Development Fund	3	Central African Republic, Guinea

Note: After 1980, American opposition based on human rights violations declined. In 1981, the United States opposed six loans to six
countries: Bolivia, Guatemala, Laos, Paraguay, Philippines, and South
Yemen. In 1982, the United States opposed six loans to three countries:
Benin, Syria, and South Yemen. The United States formally reversed
policy regarding a number of the above countries, including Argentina,
Chile, El Salvador, Guatemala, Paraguay, Philippines, South Korea, and
Uruguay. The United States opposed some loans to other countries, but
not on the basis of human rights. Source: Schoultz (1981:296-98); U.S.
House of Representatives (1983).

directly to the president of the IDB that this loan should be
rejected because Nicaragua did not have a prudent plan for
development and hence was not creditworthy. In a subsequent
letter, Shultz warned that disbursement of IDB monies to Nicaragua would "free up other monies that could be used to help
consolidate the Marxist regime and finance Nicaraguan aggres-

sion against its neighbors who are members in good standing at the Bank." Heightening the controversy, Shultz hinted that Congress would be more likely to look unfavorably on IDB replenishment should the Nicaraguan loan be approved (quoted in Friedland, 1985:2).

Members of the IDB and its president, Ortiz Mena, reacted vehemently to the American position. "When we receive a political argument, we reject it" (quoted in Friedland, 1985:2). Nicaraguan officials insisted that the United States was setting a dangerous precedent by blocking the loan. The British assistant executive director to the IDB in a memo to Britain's overseas aid agency even suggested that IDB management, under pressure from the United States concerning the Nicaraguan loan, was committing questionable actions to uphold the American position, including issuing deliberately misleading statements to the board, removing items from the agenda using unauthorized procedures, suppressing information, and removing sensitive documents on the issue from files. "This matter is open scandal, and formal protests have been lodged by, or on behalf of, every member of the board of directors except the U.S. director" (Bird and Holland, 1986:296).

Similarly, the United States was charged by Chile in 1986 with using its economic power to hold up loans to Chile for political reasons. The United States abstained on a loan request from Chile, charging that government with alleged human rights violations. The American representative stated that the abstention fulfilled a congressional requirement that the United States oppose loans to regimes found in violation of human rights standards. Chile retorted that it has been one of the most creditworthy borrowers and that American abstention violated the charter by opposing loans for political reasons. Because Canada was the only country to join the Americans in abstention, the loan was ultimately approved ("IADB Approves Borrowing by Chile as U.S. Abstains," 1986:31).

The United States has actively supported controversial policies tying American support to acceptance of its policies, as well as opposing loans on principle to certain countries for politically motivated reasons. American use of its economic hegemony has been most frequent in the IDB, and the least pervasive in the African Development Bank, where the United States has neither the voting power nor the political will to back up its position. In the case of the Asian Development Bank, officials have taken care to state that political factors do not impinge. President Takeshi Watanbe stated, "As an apolitical organization, the [Asian Development] Bank has supported and will continue to support projects regardless of the political color or the economic system of the country concerned as long as the projects meet the Bank's loan criteria" (quoted in Wilson, 1987:45). The bank was the first to make loans to Mekong Basin countries—for Cambodian electricity transmissions, Laotion agriculture, and Vietnamese fisheries (Wilson, 1987:45). So the Japanese do not appear to follow the American lead in opposing loans to countries deemed ideologically incompatible or to politically unacceptable regimes. Japan has not utilized this technique of influence.

The United States has used its economic powers by manipulating financial instruments to support specific policy preferences. In a few cases, power was blatantly exerted; most often influence was sufficient as American preferences became tied either implicitly or explicitly to contributions or withdrawal of funds. The IDB and the Asian Development Bank offer illustrative examples.

In the IDB in the mid-1980s the United States proposed changes in voting and greater use of conditionality, but cautioned that should these changes not be approved, the United States would not contribute to the replenishment of IDB resources. The United States pushed for stricter use of conditionality, arguing that the IDB was the only MDB that does not attach conditions to lending operations. The bank, according to American decision makers, should help to shape borrower's economic policies through non-project lending. The Latins argued, on the other hand, that the WB and IMF were getting a poor reputation from interfering in domestic policymaking and therefore the IDB should refrain from imposing conditionality. This proposal, like the voting initiative, was linked to an increase in replenishment. Because IDB members refused to accept conditionality, the United States reneged on replenishment.

Likewise, in the Asian Development Bank the United States has used financial techniques to show dissatisfaction with policies since 1985. To express dismay with both the progress toward privatization and with procurement procedures giving priority to local procurement over internationally competitive bidding, the United States held up contributions to the concessionary facilities (Rowley, 1985:72-73; Clad, 1986a). The effects were amplified as other donor countries followed the American lead, albeit for different reasons. In addition, the United States continued to be in arrears with its contributions to the fourth replenishment of the Asian Development Fund (1983-86), only paying the first installment. The United States, it was speculated, was "thereby gaining leverage to force its own policy prescription" (Rowley, 1985:72). American officials justified the action on the basis of economic exigencies, but as the American alternate director explained, the definition of economic criteria was broadly construed: "Economic criteria broadly include—the project, the country's economic policies, U.S. governmental policy considerations, and the applications of MDB policies and procedures to the projects" (Loong 1987:267, 269).

The strategy of being in arrears for "technical" reasons is not new; the United States has continually tried to influence the multilateral development banks by being in arrears financially. Although the situation arises in part from the timing of the congressional budgeting cycle, it also serves as an implicit warning that a reduction in American contributions could seriously jeopardize MDB operations. As far back as fiscal years 1974-77 the United States was in constant arrears to the World Bank (ranging from $335 million to $687 million a year). Both the Kassebaum Amendment, the amendment to the Foreign Relations Authorization Act of 1985, and the Gramm-Rudman Act enacted in December 1985 resulted in further arrears to United Nations-related agencies. Although the Kassebaum Amendment did not apply to the multilateral development banks, institutions that already had weighted voting, the amendment did serve as a potent reminder to the multilateral development banks of their dependency on the budgetary contributions of economic hegemons (see Williams, 1987:95-105).

The African Development Bank lacks an established economic or political hegemon. Some of the Arab regional members have the economic prowess to play such a role, especially if Egypt's purchasing of additional shares from other regional members in arrears continues. But there is no hegemonic claim, certainly no political will exercised from these states. The most vocal and active participants have been Algeria and Libya, but the latter lacks all characteristics but economic credibility, and the former has not assumed leadership. Of the sub-Saharan states, Nigeria is a likely candidate, and with the establishment of the Nigerian Trust Fund, it was anticipated that Nigeria would play such a role. Yet Nigeria has not, its economic decline diluting its hegemonic claim and its internal political state undermining consistent regional or continental leadership. At its founding, the French hoped that the Ivory Coast might play a key leadership role. During "l'affaire Fordwor," Ivorian President Félix Houphouet-Boigny, and officials H.E. Konan-Bedie and Abdoulaye Kone did try to use their prowess in support of President Fordwor—to no avail (Fordwor, 1981:66, 205). Since that episode, however, there is no concrete evidence that the Ivory Coast has attempted to wield political influence in the organization. Despite the Bank's Abidjan location and the country's relative economic strength, the Ivory Coast has played a decidedly passive role in the Bank.

In the World Bank and the Inter-American Development Bank, the United States has exerted hegemonic power in diverse ways through voting, policy initiation, and financial techniques. But with a few recent exceptions, blatant use of hegemonic instrumentalities has not been necessary. "The banks usually operate according to principles and standards which are compatible with U.S. interests, and their activities normally reflect judgments which are harmonious with basic U.S. goals in the international system" (Sanford 1982:17). When the United States has needed to use power available to a hegemon, it has been more successful when actions were couched in economic terms: "The record shows that the United States has been more successful in influencing the banks when its MDB representatives advocated new policies using the economic technical language which is the normal parlance of the multilateral banks than when they used more political terminology" (Sanford, 1982:226). When Congress has tried to place more restrictions on multilateral development bank activity—restrictions that were clearly politically motivated—American actions have met with clear resistance. Other analysts have arrived at the same conclusion as the U.S. Senate: "It would appear on the whole that Congress has had more impact on the multilateral development banks when it sought to get the administration to support certain policies than when it requires U.S. representatives to oppose loans by the banks to certain countries. The Executive branch has sometimes not fully enforced the laws governing U.S. votes in the banks, and the multilateral institutions have generally not been affected by the prohibitions contained in the U.S. legislation" (Committee on Foreign Relations, 1977:17).

In the 1980s the Japanese have been accused of exerting excessive hegemonic power in the Asian Development Bank. Because Japan is the largest contributor, the president is Japanese, and Japan wins a disproportionate share of procurement contracts, the bank is described as "being Japanese." Although Japanese influence is strong, Japanese domination is, in the words of Dick Wilson, "a wild exaggeration."

The Japanese stake is still relatively small compared to all the others, and a Japanese President would have to be superhuman to overcome the combined wishes of all the other large and vocal powers who belong to the Bank. . . . Nor are the Japanese corporations, contrary to some beliefs, hogging a disproportionately large amount of the procurement business for Bank contracts. . . . What makes the Bank so interesting is precisely the fact that neither the Americans nor the Japanese nor anyone else controls or manipulates it in the way that has happened in some other institutions. Both the United States and Japan are rather small shareholders in the wider scheme of Bank membership. [Wilson, 1987:356-57]

Evaluating the significance of hegemonic power is a difficult undertaking. Hegemons have used a variety of techniques, in-

cluding influencing contributions and hence votes, manipulating financial instrumentalities, and supporting specific policies. The use of such techniques has brought them into conflict
with other members. These techniques are not neutral as functionalist theory would portend. But wielding hegemonic policy
instruments does not necessarily lead to hegemonic control.
Although all policies within the multilateral development
banks have not been congruent to, or compatible with, hegemonic interests, American power has had a very significant
effect on both the World Bank and the Inter-American Development Bank, a moderately significant effect on the Asian Development Bank, and virtually no impact on the African Development Bank even though the adhesion of extraregional
hegemons generated fear of hegemonic dominance. But
hegemons are not the only actors responsible for political conflict.

Interorganizational Politics

Politics emerges from the competition for scarce resources.
Three types of interorganizational competition are particularly
relevant: among member countries for the purportedly scarce
economic resources of the economic institution; among donor
states for "capturing" the clientele of recipient states, including
procurement contracts; and among competing international
organizations for funding the best potential projects. All the
banks utilize essentially the same procedures to organize the
competition, but the outcome of the competition has been
different.

Officials in each bank have been sensitive to the need to
distribute resources (largely projects) among the various borrowing country members. Many, including the African Development Bank, have adopted the goal of at least one project per
country per year. The Asian Development Bank has been particularly cognizant of the importance of resource allocation, but
its formula for allocation has generated controversy.

The Asian Development Bank gave special regard for smaller
countries of Asia in the founding charter. That was one reason

why India, already a major World Bank beneficiary, chose not to borrow from the Asian institution. The founders were concerned that relatively too much money was already going to members of the British Commonwealth and not to other Asian nations. Historically some countries have benefited from Asian Development Bank assistance more than others. Almost half of the twenty-year cumulative total was taken by the three largest borrowers, Indonesia (19%), Pakistan (16%), and the Philippines (12%). And although the absolute amounts have accounted for only 2% of total money lent by the bank, the Pacific Islands have received about one and a half times more aid per head from the bank than other members have received. This apparent discrepancy is controversial. President Masao Fujioka has been accused of having "a reparations mentality. He just wants to shovel the money out" (Clad, 1986b:61).

Two other issues of distribution of resources have also catapulted to the top of the Asian Development Bank's organizational agenda: the question of "graduation" and the new competition caused by the People's Republic of China and India. Bank officials have argued against graduation for the more developed members of Hong Kong and Singapore, fearing that these members might lose interest in the bank. So these two countries still borrow despite their economic success (Wilson, 1987:277). Yet if both China, which joined the bank in 1986, and India, which announced in the same year that it would begin to borrow, submitted many projects, bank officials fear that efforts in other countries by economic necessity would be diluted (Wilson, 1987:275). So the competition over scarce funds is likely to become stiffer in the Asian Development Bank, as norms against "big country" borrowing are challenged and countries refuse to graduate from recipient to donor status.

In contrast, in the African Development Bank, with the augmentation of economic resources caused by the adhesion of the extraregionals, loan competition may have decreased. Bank officials, however, remain cognizant of the need to distribute funds to all regional borrowing members and to try to meet the informal quota of one project per country annually. But regional shares have not been equal—East and West African states'

Table 18. Procurement by the Multilateral Development
Banks (cumulative shares by % of total)

IBRD		IDA	
United States	22.6	United States	14.0
Japan	15.9	United Kingdom	14.0
Fed. Rep. of Germany	12.5	Japan	14.9
France	7.2	Fed. Rep. of Germany	11.3
United Kingdom	8.6	France	9.1
Cumulative percentages through 30 June 1985.			

Asian Development Bank		African Development Bank	
Japan	25.7	France	19.0
S. Korea	11.8	Fed. Rep. of Germany	10.8
U.S.	8.3	United Kingdom	9.3
Fed. Rep. of Germany	5.5	Italy	8.3
Philippines	5.4	United States	4.2
Cumulative percentages through end of 1986.			

Sources: World Bank. *Annual Report* (1986); Asian Development
Bank. *Quarterly Procurement Statistics* (1987); ADB Planning and Research Department. *Compendium of Statistics* (1987).

shares (seventeen and fifteen states, respectively) have declined,
while those to Central and North Africa states (eleven and seven
states, respectively) have increased. If funds become more restricted and West and East African states fail to qualify for loans
either because of loan arrears or informal cross-conditionality,
then the maldistribution of loans may become a more controversial issue.

Donors compete, too, not only for general influence, shares,
or votes, but also for "capturing" the clientele of recipient states
through procurement contracts. There is a long-standing perception that the United States receives a disproportionate share
of procurement in the World Bank and Inter-American Development Bank, that Japan receives a disproportionate share in the
Asian Development Bank, and France in the African Development Bank.

Table 18 reports the procurement figures. The expectation of
American dominance in procurement is not confirmed for the
World Bank group, 22.6% in the IBRD and only 14.0% in IDA.

Procurement figures are not even released by the Inter-American Development Bank probably because of fear of repercussions from countries dissatisfied with disproportionate procurement from the United States.

Over the twenty-year period of the Asian Development Bank's lending, Japan has received 25.7% of total procurement, South Korea 11.8%, and the United States 8.3% (Asian Development Bank, *Quarterly Procurement Statistics* 1987). There is considerable evidence that procurement specifications have been tailored to Japanese products. For example, in 1979 an Asian Development Bank evaluation of a South Korean fishing project reported that "diesel specifications have been written precisely around" a type of Japanese engine. The report acknowledged that "procurement procedures were not followed" (Clad, 1986b:61). However, the trend may be changing due both to the appreciation of the yen and to increasing competition from Asia's own newly industrializing powers. In 1986, the same year American officials criticized the number of Japanese contracts, Japan received only 15% of procurement. Furthermore, the bank introduced a 15% preference for developing countries in procurement of goods, together with a 7.5% preference for civil works awards. Because many American officials opposed preferential rather than internationally competitive bidding, the procurement issue is still a controversial one (Rogers, 1986).

Similar accusations have been levelled against French procurement (19.0% of total) in the African Development Bank. Historic colonial ties to France, France's record in training African technical experts used to working with products manufactured in the former colonial power, and the French government's critical role (a "monumental effort") to support French enterprise all result in French procurement. When contracts are let, they are often written expressly for French equipment using French specifications. And the government, more than any other donor government, supports French enterprises by helping them receive procurement.

In all cases, allegations of preferential procurement have been met with anger from other donors hoping to have benefited financially from procurement contracts. The financial rewards from procurement may be substantial if the estimates made by the Asian Development Bank are accurate: roughly 84% of the bank's total expenditure is for procuring goods, equipment, and civil works, with another 6% for consulting services (Wilson, 1987:255). Donors have alot to gain (and to lose) in procurement politics.

Finally, the organizations themselves compete in inter-organizational politics for funds and personnel. As the organizations become more established, secretariats are increasingly able to act as autonomous actors. The extent to which the various development banks have achieved organizational autonomy, and therefore are able to act as independent political agents, varies. Under the leadership of Robert McNamara, the World Bank achieved this autonomy, extricating itself from the direct control of the United States government (Ascher, 1990). Compared to the other banks, the World Bank has acted the most autonomously. With a professional staff of over 3,000 individuals, the World Bank has developed procedures and expertise that separate it from member states. Decisions of World Bank staff and management on both project specifics and policy advice have been increasingly taken with little input from the executive directors (Ascher, 1983:421). Despite the directors' official oversight responsibility, the board chooses to veto projects under only the most extraordinary circumstances. They discuss the more general (and admittedly most important issues), while a professional, quasi-autonomous staff implements the decisions.

None of the other banks has achieved such organizational autonomy. The executive directors representing state members play a much more critical role. As these organizations become more experienced and are able to attract the highly professionally qualified staff, there is apt to be more interorganizational competition. The Asian Development Bank has felt keenly competition from the World Bank in terms of personnel (high turnover [17% at end of 1970s] attributed in part to personnel joining the World Bank) and projects (where World Bank financed the big projects; "small business" and South Pacific being the preserve of the Asian Bank) (Wilson, 1987:78, 108-9, 275).

Interorganizational politics is relevant for the relationship between the World Bank and each of the regional development institutions. Each of these pair of banks is involved in cofinancing of projects that bring them into direct contact with each other. With increased cofinancing, two politically sensitive issues have been placed on the agenda of each: cross-conditionality and debt rescheduling. For the Asian Development Bank, these two issues are already controversial. Commercial banks, a major source of cofinancing with the Asian Development Bank, tend to require mandatory cross-default clauses, so the bank and its cofinanciers find themselves immediately at odds. The bank claims that it has been unwilling to accept such provisions (Wilson, 1987:250). To avoid embroilment in the controversy, the bank follows a policy of not getting involved in debt rescheduling. But as Eduardo Lizano, an official of the Inter-American Development Bank, laments, although the IDB has not yet participated in cross-conditionality, "the forces and pressures for changing this situation are well-known." It is harder for the regional development banks not to get involved because as cofinanciers they may have a minor role (Dell, 1988:566).

Intraorganizational Politics

Intraorganizational politics occurs as a result of controversial management decisions made in the bank. Dissenters opine that such decisions are either outside the competence of the organization or blatantly political. Accusations against management may become more heated if there are charges of mismanagement of resources. Part of the task of the evaluation process is to assess the propriety and effectiveness of management and to uncover malfeasance.

The case of the World Bank's move to poverty-oriented projects illustrates a change, largely undertaken by management, that erupted in political controversy. As Robert Ayres graphically portrays:

a number of political controversies, tensions, and contradictions were generated within the institution. There were many Bank officers who were not wildly enthusiastic about the poverty-related reorientations of lending, and they came into conflict with those of their colleagues desiring to move more rapidly into anti-poverty initiatives. The politics of implementing poverty-oriented development projects therefore largely involved organizational and programmatic conflicts within an institution experiencing some abrupt changes in the definition of its tasks. There were many bureaucratic turf struggles, generational discrepancies, debates between theorists and practitioners, contrasting viewpoints on agricultural development, equally contrasting viewpoints about employment generation and so forth. [1983:209]

Instances of possible mismanagement have also generated political conflict in both the Asian Development Bank and the African Development Bank. President Fujioka, elected to a second term in the Asian bank in 1986, has been accused of trying to keep disbursement rates increasing annually by supporting uneconomic loans. James Clad reports,

Many professional staff and [Asian Development Bank] board members contacted by the [Far Eastern Economic Review] charged that project facts are frequently tailored to justify lending. They also said a growing number of project approvals have involved glaring departures from long-standing bank policies. Directors spoke of "sloppiness" in bank documentation.

More seriously, some staffers charged that deliberate distortion of facts and invention of data has occurred to suit the annual loan-approval timetable (invariably bunched in the last quarter of the calendar year). And, in contravention of the [Asian Development Bank's] charter, they said management has sometimes advanced overtly political reason to justify lending. One senior economist says "about one-third of the projects are cooked in one way or another." [1986b:60]

Specific examples of such practices have been documented. To meet an "informal quota" on number of projects approved, bank officials approved a loan to Pakistan, although aware that cofinancing had not yet been arranged. Officials lent money for an Indian electric project cognizant of the large subsidy for electricity rates—a policy clearly contrary to Asian Development Bank procedures. Loans were given to Nepal, although the borrower was known to be "technically bankrupt" (Clad, 1986b:60-61). Internal investigations of these allegations have proceeded. But bank management has reportedly punished individuals or threatened to demote those "leaking" information on mismanagement charges. Such investigations are particularly sensitive, as they impinge on the purported "cult of personality" surrounding the president (Clad, 1986b:61).

As reported in chapter 2, President Fordwor of the African Development Bank was not preserved by the cult of personality. He was charged by the executive directors with making unilateral decisions on personnel and financial regulations, without constitutionally mandated consultation with the executive directors. Accused of being the major "player" in the ADB and not a neutral participant, he resigned (Fordwor, 1981). Subsequent presidents have devoted considerable attention to professionalizing the staff and institutionalizing procedures so that similar accusations of mismanagement do not occur. The election in 1985 of an ADB professional and a financial expert, Babacar N'Diaye, to the presidency suggests the importance members now attribute to professionalism.

Allegations of impropriety have also arisen in the Asian Development Bank because of the dominant role played by Japanese personnel in the bank. Along with the president, the director of budget, personnel, and management is always Japanese. About 10% of the professional staff are also from Japan. The fact that these Japanese have heretofore played a relatively low profile tends to soften criticism of Japanese dominance, as does the fact that 10% of the bank's professional staff are American and over one-quarter of its personnel have studied in the United States (Wilson, 1987:282, 302-3).

Post hoc evaluations of projects discussed in chapter 9 are one procedure designed to signal mismanagement of projects. Initially viewed as an internal management technique, African Development Bank evaluations have typically focused on the Bank's performance in achieving the economic rate of return on a project forecast at appraisal. But the review is incomplete. Performance by borrowing country governments is not systematically evaluated or if shortcomings are found, they go unreported due to the sensitivity of interorganizational relations. And external contractors for projects, although their performance is evaluated, almost never receive copies of the post hoc evaluation. Under these procedures for post hoc evaluations, only gross mismanagement is uncovered. Both the World Bank's process for evaluation and that bank's management performance remain the models to emulate.

With a couple of prominent exceptions, charges of gross mismanagement have not adversely affected the banks. Mismanagement has not significantly created or exacerbated political controversy, particularly compared to mismanagement charges within other international governmental organizations like the United Nations Education, Scientific, and Cultural Organization, the Food and Agriculture Organization, or the Organization of African Unity. But such charges do periodically undermine the bank's performance. The charges become particularly inflammatory when they coincide with policy changes opposed by some members of the respective banks or personnel within the banks.

The Issue of Conditionality

The issue of conditionality permits us to examine the relationship among the three arenas where conflicts occur. The United States government has been a long-time advocate of conditionality as historically practiced in the International Monetary Fund. It pushed for greater use of conditionality in the World Bank. By the late 1970s, in the aftermath of the two oil shocks, the United States and World Bank officials acting together concluded that the bank needed to link disbursement of funds and concern for policy issues (Please, 1984:24). As a result, in 1980 the World Bank introduced the new program of Structural Adjustment Lending (SAL) described in chapter 8. The hegemon supported strongly the notion of conditionality, and after 1980 the policy became an integral component of World Bank strategy.

The symbiosis between the United States and the World Bank developed in part because of American pressure on the institution. Equally as important, however, seems to have been independent recognition by World Bank officials that as general economic decline set in, as it did in the 1970s, the bank had to alter its approach. Even though the bank provides only a relatively small proportion of total external flows (6%-7%), the most severely affected states are the most heavily influenced by multilateral capital infusion. And many of these states are in dire need of policy reform. The fact that the United States was ready to implement cross-conditionality served to reemphasize the symbiotic relationship on the issue of conditionality.

Increased use of conditionality by the International Monetary Fund and the World Bank has clearly undermined the functional roots and economic neutrality of the international financial institutions. Intraorganizational disputes have arisen not over whether conditionality should be utilized, but over what the specific conditions should be and the appropriate timetable for compliance. Country experts tended to be more lenient, seeking looser conditionalities on an extended timetable, whereas functional experts argued for stricter adherence to "tough" guidelines. Interorganizational "turf" battles developed over the appropriate role of the IMF and World Bank, as discussed in chapter 8.

Most acute has been interorganizational controversy between the World Bank and the regional development banks over the conditionality issue. Both World Bank officials and the United States as important donors in all the organizations have pressured the regional banks to tie lending to particular policy reforms. In the Inter-American Development Bank, the United States, much to the dismay of Latin American members, has tried to convince other members to support policy changes. However, the debt crisis in Brazil, Argentina, and Mexico has forced the IDB to reexamine its opposition to policy advice and specific conditionality.

According to the logic of the Baker Plan, proposed at the annual joint meeting of the World Bank and IMF in 1985 in Seoul, the debt crisis can only be resolved through sustained growth for debtor countries. To achieve the objective, economic reform is required, including the elimination of state subsidies and the termination of price controls, increased reliance on the private sector, and export promotion and trade liberalization (Hakim, 1986:55). Along with the World Bank, the IDB is singled out as an essential institution for providing new sources of capital to debtor countries, thanks to the expected influx of capital from the United States. Thus under the Baker Plan, the multilateral development banks and the IDB (and the Asian Development Bank to a lesser extent) are to play a key role in financing growth. Economic reform negotiated between borrowers and bank officials is to be a vital component of the policy package—a package that specifies changes in governmental policy. The Baker Plan depended, however, not only on domestic economic reform, but on a massive influx of American economic resources. Yet "Neither the carrot of regulatory changes which might have prompted greater commercial bank cooperation, nor the stick of sustained pressure has materialized. No mechanisms have yet been created for implementing the Baker Plan. No procedures have been formulated for debtor countries to secure the promised new loans" (Hakim, 1986:56). The African Development Bank was not even mentioned in the Baker Plan, although the Bank has become involved in the question of policy advice, as described in chapter 5.

The Asian Development Bank seems to have been affected least by the conditionality issue. The region as a whole suffered the least from the downturn in economic fortunes, and indeed, a number of the bank's members capitalized on the changes in the international division of labor. South Korea, Japan, Taiwan, and Singapore all enjoyed very high rates of economic growth, whereas the growth rates of many African countries actually declined. As a result, the Asian Development Bank has been able to assume a rather pragmatic position on offering policy advice, issuing such advice periodically, and then only with reluctance—much to the chagrin of the United States.

From a substantive and procedural viewpoint, what worries most borrowing country members of the regional development banks about the increasing similarity of WB and IMF approach to conditionality is the specter of either formal or informal cross-conditionality. The fear is legitimate if the regional banks

Table 19. Arenas of Political Conflict in the Multilateral
        Development Banks: A Comparative Analysis

Arenas of Politics	World Bank	African Dev. Bank	Inter-Amer. Dev. Bank	Asian Dev. Bank
1. Hegemonic				
contributions/votes	+ +	–	+ +	+
policies	+ +	–	+ +	+
manipulating				
finances	+ +	–	+ +	+
2. Interorganizational	–	+	+ +	+ +
3. Intraorganizational	+	+	–	+ +

Key: + + Very significant levels of political conflict; + Moderately
significant levels of political conflict; – Relatively insignificant levels
of political conflict.

support conditionality policies. The regional banks' reticence
to support strong conditionality has raised the level of political
conflict among various constituencies of the respective banks.
Thus hegemonic initiatives and interorganizational (WB and
IMF) and intraorganizational pressures on the conditionality
issue have each contributed to making the banks' political institutions.

Comparing Political Arenas in the
Multilateral Development Banks

In table 19 the relative significance of political factors in each
of the three arenas is compared for the multilateral development
banks. Hegemonic politics appears to be the most pervasive. In
the World Bank and Inter-American Development Bank,
hegemonic politics has had a very significant effect and in the
Asian Development Bank a lesser effect—irrespective of whether or how the hegemon employs contributions or votes, policies,
or manipulation of financial instrumentalities. The United
States exercised its hegemonic power in the World Bank and
Inter-American Development Bank and the persistent conflict
between an ascendant Japan and the United States exacerbated

conflict in the Asian Development Bank. What makes the African Development Bank unique is that in the absence of an acknowledged hegemon, the Bank is relatively insulated from hegemonic politics.

Interorganizational relations have been particularly affected by the donor community's attempts to push the multilateral development banks toward reshaping recipient governments' economic policies. World Bank officials, largely the architects of such policy, can, as the dominant institution, ignore interorganizational politics; the Inter-American Development Bank and the Asian Development Bank cannot. Both organizations have been subject to the most direct and persistent donor efforts to intervene in regional members' affairs in the direction of economic liberalization and increased privatization. In addition, both organizations have experienced conflict over resource allocation, emanating from the fact that in both Latin America and Asia, the largest countries, including India, Brazil, and Mexico, receive a disproportionate share of World Bank funding. Because of this perceived inequity, there is constant debate over allocation of resources—whether World Bank funding should substitute for regional development funds. Finally, in both organizations there is a clear perception of direct competition with the World Bank for competent personnel.

Of the regional development banks, the African Development Bank has experienced relatively less interorganizational politics than either the Inter-American Development Bank or the Asian Development Bank has. Competition still exists (hence, the moderately significant rating). Because the African Development Bank until recently has been viewed as weaker financially, and hence less capable—indeed, less competitive with the other development finance institutions—interorganizational politics may be relatively less salient.

Political controversy emanating from intraorganizational sources has been relatively insignificant in the Inter-American Development Bank at least since the 1970s. The bank itself has proposed no new policy initiatives and allegations of gross mismanagement have not surfaced. In contrast, by the mid-1980s, the Asian Development Bank seems to have experienced the highest levels of political conflict in this arena. Controversy over proposed policy changes, fueled by the American stance on privatization, coupled with the troubled tenure of President Fujioka and alleged charges of mismanagement under his leadership, have sparked high levels of animosity—hence, the "very significant" rating. Intraorganizational politics in the World Bank and the African Development Bank falls into the middle range.

This comparative examination of arenas of political conflict suggests that the Asian Development Bank and the Inter-American Development have experienced the highest levels of political conflict. And the African Development Bank, largely because of the absence of a hegemon exercising power, has encountered the least. This finding tends to confirm the view that while all these organizations are political institutions, in the absence of a hegemon, political conflict is relatively less pervasive.

Conclusion

Infusion of politics is clearly inimical to the doctrine of functionalism generally or economic neutrality espoused in the various charters of the multilateral development banks. This study has shown that political factors have intervened in all the development banks, with the African Development Bank experiencing the least significant levels. This finding does not, however, mean that the ADB is the most effective of the multilateral development banks. Although very significant levels of political conflict may be deleterious, some political controversy may be advantageous at least for some of the participants. As Kwame Donkoh Fordwor suggests, "there are situations in which a cherished and legitimate objective cannot be achieved except by resort to political action or political leverage" (1981:xiv). Five advantages of the international financial institutions being political, not economically neutral, functional organizations are discussed below.

First, hegemonic politics, irrespective of the specific technique utilized, may have beneficial effects for the smaller and weaker members. As long as the hegemon's nominal political objectives are met, a hegemonic power may be less likely to exert control, keeping its hegemonic power in reserve for use at critical times. Under such conditions, even if political issues intervene, other state members, especially weaker developing countries, may actually have greater flexibility to pursue their own interests within the parameters established by the hegemon. As Stephen D. Krasner argues, "For the weak, hegemony provides room for maneuver within the broad milieu goals of the dominant state" (1981:305). As long as hegemonic dominance is assured, hegemons may be more willing to contribute additional financing. Should the weaker powers try to alter the basic framework, fundamentally challenging hegemonic power, then the hegemon will be more apt to diminish or even withdraw financial and political support.

Second, interorganizational political competition may be healthy. For example, the competition between the World Bank and the African Development Bank for supporting the best "most doable" projects has forced the ADB to expand donor-funded preinvestment surveys, to become more involved in shaping individual project proposals, and to submit appraisal reports acceptable to the scrupulous eyes of the extraregional executive directors. To recruit the services of capable officials in the international civil service, the ADB has had to offer comparable salaries, to develop a rudimentary career service system, and to expand benefits in order to assure a competitive environment for personnel. Interorganizational competition has forced the ADB to change to maintain a competitive position.

Third, intraorganizational politics may in the long term lead to new policies and curb mismanagement. New policies adopted as a result of political pressures may, in fact, be more suitable policies. The reemphasis on projects for the basic needs of the poor in the 1970s is such as example. New items are added to the political agenda, where controversies are debated and new decisions are made. By calling attention to mismanagement, ideally, the practices should be curbed.

Fourth, when international economic institutions nudge recipients to accept conditionality, direct intervention by the

multilateral development banks in a borrower's economic affairs, states may be taking actions that are in the government's
long-term economic interests. In a few cases, such intervention
(or in the case of Nigeria, the rejection of IMF funds contingent
on the implementation of austerity measures) may have permitted the leadership to undertake politically unpopular unilateral
austerity measures that they could not have done without the
pressure of conditionality (Harden, 1987:18-19). The potential
long-term benefit is that the political measures supported by
the development agencies for economic reasons may strengthen
the country economically.

Fifth, political conflict may be a radical alternative utilized
by weaker members to alter norms or procedures under which
the organization was established. Persisting conflict may have
so eroded the norms of power as to leave the whole institution
vulnerable to change. Political conflict may be the only avenue
for counterhegemonic forces to organize countervailing power.
This study of the MDBs and the ADB in particular suggests
neither that such a level of political conflict exists nor that
counterhegemons want to alter the system fundamentally.

Very significant levels of political conflict can, however, be
counterproductive, if not deleterious. Hegemonic politics may
jeopardize the legitimacy of the organization as an independent
institution. Periods of American control over the World Bank in
the 1950s and 1960s were leading in this direction, until bank
officials in greater numbers and with acknowledged expertise
acted more autonomously, muting American influence and the
power of the executive directors more generally. How often and
to what extent the hegemon can exert its influence without
encountering adverse effects is unknown. Indeed, the threshold
may be different for each institution. If the hegemon uses power
without restraint to control the agenda and the purse strings,
then the organization may be seen as only a political instrument
of the hegemon and its legitimacy diminished. American power
and influence in the Inter-American Development Bank may
have reached this point prior to the late 1970s.

On the other hand, the decline of the hegemon may not
necessarily lead to diminished political conflict or a reinstate-

ment of functionalism. Krasner asserts, "Normal powers are more likely to be concerned with clearly identifiable, shorter-term political and economic objectives. They will not contribute substantial resources to an international organization whose operational decisions are beyond their control" (1981: 305). American policy in the Inter-American Development Bank and the Asian Development Bank may have reached this stalemate. The United States' attempt in the mid-1980s to garner more voting control in the IDB is illustrative, as is America's antagonistic response to Japan's newly exercised power in the Asian Development Bank. Even the absence of a hegemon in the African Development Bank only leads to political conflict in other arenas.

Intraorganizational politics may also be disadvantageous if it results in either unpopular or unworkable management policy decisions or if charges of mismanagement have never been satisfactorily resolved. The American effort to push privatization is a clear example of the first case. There continues to be persistent, potentially disabling controversy concerning the efficacy of such an approach. Should American funding be coupled more directly with the privatization issue, the long-term efforts on the organization's continued viability could be devastating. In the second case, if political interests block investigation of allegations of mismanagement or if mismanagement practices are not corrected, then political conflict may not only have short-term negative consequences, but it may have exacerbated organizational problems in the long term.

The doctrine of economic neutrality provides the ideological foundation of the banks, but its veracity has proven short lived. What both member states and the organization's leadership must be cognizant of are the benefits and liabilities to them and to the international organization of different arenas and levels of political conflict.

At its founding, the African Development Bank tried to prevent hegemonic politics by limiting its membership to regional members. Hegemonic politics was minimized and inter-organizational rivalries muted due to the ADB's lack of resources. Political conflict still existed, however, as the result of management decisions and mismanagement. At the beginning of the 1980s, the decision to admit extraregional members profoundly altered the organization. The augmentation of economic (and hence political) resources resulted in increased pressure to intervene more decisively in member states' economic decisions and in increased interorganizational rivalry.

The uniqueness of the case of the African Development Bank is that the hegemons who have played such a key role in the other banks and have exercised such political influence have both been prevented from exercising inordinate influence through limitations on contributions and have, themselves, chosen to curb their political and economic influence. The relative absence of hegemonic politics may sustain the legitimacy of the African Development Bank as it confronts the stark realities of the 1990s. But even in the absence of a hegemon, the roots of political conflict through intraorganizational and interorganizational arenas penetrate deep into the various modes of international governance including international organizations.

Works Cited

African Development Bank. 1976. *Nigeria Trust Fund Agreement between the Federal Republic of Nigeria and the African Development Bank for the Establishment of the Nigeria Trust Fund.*

———. 1978. *Major Issues Concerning the Opening of ADB's Capital Stock to Non-Regional States* (A Working Paper). November.

———. 1979a. *Letter from Dr. Horst Moltrecht, the Coordinator of the Nonregional States Transmitting the Position Paper of the Nonregional States Invited to Participate in the African Development Bank.* London. 14 February.

———. 1979b. *Report on Consultations Held between the African Development Bank and Non-Regional States Concerning Their Possible Membership in the Bank.* Abidjan. February.

———. 1981a. *Agreement Establishing the African Development Bank.*

———. 1981b. *Staff Manual.* 31 December.

———. 1983. *General Conditions Applicable to Loan and Guarantee Agreements.*

———. 1984a. *The ADB Group's Contribution to the Implementation of the Panafrican Telecommunications Network.* 30 May.

———. 1984b. "Critical Analysis of the Application of Sanctions to Arrears on ADB Loans" (ADB/BD/WL/84/42). 22 March.

———. 1984c. *Étude Économique Sur les Comoroes.*

———. 1984d. *Manual of Operating Procedures.*

———. 1985a. "Directives Relating to the Recovery of Arrears on Loans Granted By ADB" (ADB/ADF/BD/FC/85/01).

———. 1985b. *Ethiopia: Economic Prospects and Country Programming* OCRN II. February.

———. Various years. *Appraisal Reports.* Various countries.

ADB Evaluation Division. 1984. *Abstract of Evaluation Reports* No. 1. May.

ADB Planning and Research Department. 1981. "Functions and Responsibilities of the Evaluation Division." November.

————. 1982. *Étude d'évaluation des lignes de crédit de la BAD accordées à l'Industrial Development Bank du Kenya et Tanzania Investment Bank* (ADB/PLR/82/02).

————. 1983. *Energy Policy and Planning in Africa,* by W.F. Steel, A.E. N'Diaye, O.M.B. Kariisa and D. Kohler. June. Economic Research Paper no. 1.

————. 1984a. *Exchange Rates and the Management of the External Sector in Sub-Saharan Africa,* by D.G. Rwegasina. April. Economic Research Paper no. 3.

————. 1984b. *The Future Role of the African Development Bank in Promoting Economic Development and Social Progress in Africa,* by M.V. Mwamufiya. May. Economic Research Report no. 4

————. 1985. *Post-Evaluation Report on the Banjul Yundum International Airport Phase II Development Project in the Gambia.* September.

————. 1987, 1984. *Compendium of Statistics.* Statistics Division.

African Development Bank/African Development Fund, Board of Governors. Various years. *Annual Report.*

————. Various years. *Summary Records,* Annual Meetings.

ADB, Battelle, Geneva Research Centre. 1984. *Symposium on Regional Development Projects in West Africa. Preparatory Report.* April.

African Development Bank–Economic Commission for Africa. 1983. *ECA and Africa's Development, 1983-2008: A Preliminary Perspective Study.* Addis Ababa: ECA. April.

African Development Bank Group. 1981. *Roles and Policies of Multilateral Development Banks. Responses to Queries by the United States Treasury Department.* June.

African Development Bank, United States Agency for International Development. 1980. *Evaluation Report of the AID Regular and Special Sahel Grants,* Report Text. May.

African Development Fund. Various years. *Appraisal Reports.* Various countries. *Africa Recovery.* Various issues.

Afrique. 1983. No. 1149 (12 Jan.): 45.

Aiken, M., and J. Hage. 1978. "Organizational Interdependence and Intra-Organizational Structure." In *Interorganizational Relations, Selected Readings,* ed. William M. Evan, pp. 161-84. Philadelphia: Univ. of Pennsylvania Press.

Aldrich, Howard. 1979. *Organizations and Environments.* Englewood Cliffs, N.J.: Prentice-Hall.

Aldrich, Howard, and D.A. Whetton. 1981. "Organization-Sets, Action-Sets and Networks: Making the Most Out of Simplicity." In *Handbook of Organizational Design*, vol. 1, ed. P.C. Nystrom and W.H. Starbuck, pp. 385-408. New York: Oxford Univ. Press.

Amégavie, Yewon Charles. 1977. *La Banque Africaine de Développement*. Paris: Pedone.

Amuzegar, Jabangir. 1986. "The IMF under Fire." *Foreign Policy* no. 64 (Fall): 98-119.

Arnold, Steven H. 1982. *Implementing Development Assistance. European Approaches to Basic Needs*. Boulder: Westview.

Ascher, William. 1983. "New Development Approaches and the Adaptability of International Agencies: The Case of the World Bank." *International Organization* 37, no. 3 (Summer): 415-39.

————. 1990. "The World Bank and U.S. Control." In *The United States and Multilateral Institutions: Patterns of Changing Instrumentality and Influence*, ed. Margaret P. Karns and Karen A. Mingst, pp. 115-39. Boston: Unwin Hyman.

Asian Development Bank. Various years. *Annual Report*.

————. Various years. *Quarterly Procurement Statistics*.

Assetto, Valerie J. 1986. "Crisis and Innovation in the IMF." Paper prepared for the annual meeting of the International Studies Association, Anaheim, Calif., 25-29 March.

Ayres, Robert. 1983. *Banking on the Poor: The World Bank and World Poverty*. Cambridge: MIT Press.

Baldwin, David A. 1965. "The International Bank in Political Perspective." *World Politics* 18 (October): 68-81.

————. 1985. *Economic Statecraft*. Princeton: Princeton Univ. Press.

Baum, Warren, and Stokes M. Tolbert. 1985. *Investing in Development. Lessons of World Bank Experience*. New York: Oxford Univ. Press.

Bendo-Soupou, Dominique. 1985. "L'ouverture de la stratégie de la Banque Africaine de Développement à travers son capital-actions." *Le Mois en Afrique* (Paris), no. 227-28 (January): 55-99.

Berg, Robert J. 1986. "Foreign Aid in Africa: Here's the Answer—Is It Relevant to the Question?" In *Strategies for African Development*, ed. R.J. Berg and J. Whitaker, pp. 505-43. Berkeley: Univ. of California Press.

Bird, Kai, and Max Holland. 1985. "Nicaragua: No Friend at the I.D.B." *The Nation* 240 (March): 231.

————. 1986. "The Unilateralists." *The Nation* 242 (15 March): 296.

Blackburn, Peter. 1985. "Disappointing 1984 Raises Questions for Future." *Africa Economic Digest* (15 April): 14.

Brooke, James. 1987. "African Bank Leaders to Meet." *New York Times* (1 June), IV:14.

Callaghy, Thomas M. 1987. "Between Scylla and Charybdis: The Foreign Economic Relations of Sub-Saharan African States." *Annals of the American Academy of Political and Social Science* 489 (January): 148-63.

"Change at the ADB." 1985. *West Africa* (20 May): 979-85.

Clad, James. 1986a. "Last-Resort Lender." *Far Eastern Economic Review* 132 (15 May): 64-65.

———. 1986b. "Unhappy Returns." *Far Eastern Economic Review* 134 (27 November): 60-63.

Clark, John F. 1979. "Patterns of Support for International Organizations in Africa." In *The Politics of Africa: Dependence and Development*, ed. Timothy M. Shaw and Kenneth A. Heard, pp. 319-55. New York: Africana Publishing.

Cox, Robert W. 1980. "The Crisis of World Order and the Problem of International Organizations in the 1980s." *International Journal* 35 (Spring): 370-95.

Daltrop, Anne. 1986. *Politics and the European Community.* London: Longman.

Dell, Sidney. 1972. *The Inter-American Development Bank: A Study in Development Financing.* New York: Praeger.

———. 1988. "The Question of Cross-Conditionality." *World Development* 16 (5): 557-68.

DeWitt, R. Peter. 1987. "Policy Directions in International Lending, 1961-1984: The Case of the Inter-American Development Bank." *Journal of Developing Areas* 21 (April): 277-84.

DeWitt, R. Peter, Jr. 1977. *The Inter-American Development Bank and Political Influence: With Special Reference to Costa Rica.* New York: Praeger.

Evan, William. 1978. "An Organization-Set Model of Interorganizational Relations." In *Interorganizational Relations: Selected Readings*, ed. William M. Evan, pp. 78-90. Philadelphia: Univ. of Pennsylvania Press.

Finkelstein, Lawrence, ed. 1988. *Politics in the United Nations System.* Durham, N.C.: Duke Univ. Press.

Fisher, Bart S. 1972. *The International Coffee Agreement: A Study in Coffee Diplomacy.* New York: Praeger.

Fordwor, Kwame Donkoh. 1981. *The African Development Bank: Problems of International Cooperation.* New York: Pergamon Press.

Frenkel, Roberto, and Guillermo O'Donnell. 1979. "The 'Stabilization Programs' of the International Monetary Fund and Their Internal Impacts." In *Capitalism and the State in U.S.-Latin American Relations*, ed. Richard R. Fagen, pp. 171-216. Stanford, Ca.: Stanford Univ. Press.

Friedland, Jonathan. 1985. "Debt Fears Waning, Politics Heating Up as Development Bank Meets in Vienna." *American Banker* 152 (25 March): 2, 7.

———. 1987. "Conflict Looms as Latin Bank Members Meet." *American Banker* 152 (23 March): 2.

Friedman, Irving S. 1984. *Report on Financial Policies of the African Development Bank*. Consultant Report. 12 April.

"Gâchis à Addis Ababa." 1985. *Jeune Afrique* 1294 (23 October): 11-17.

Gardiner, Robert K.A., and Pickett, James. 1984. *The African Development Bank, 1964-1984: An Experiment in Economic Co-operation and Development*. Abidjan: African Development Bank.

Girling, Robert Henriques. 1985. *Multinational Institutions and the Third World: Management, Debt, and Trade Conflicts in the International Economic Order*. New York: Praeger.

Gordenker, Leon. 1976. *International Aid and National Decisions: Development Programs in Malawi, Tanzania, and Zambia*. Princeton: Princeton Univ. Press.

Gordon, David F., and Joan C. Parker. 1984. "The World Bank and Its Critics: The Case of Sub-Saharan Africa." *Discussion Paper, University of Michigan, Center for Research on Economic Development* 108 (March): 9-12.

Green, Reginald Herbold, and Caroline Allison. 1986. "The World Bank's Agenda for Accelerated Development: Dialectics, Doubts and Dialogues." In *Africa in Economic Crisis*, ed. John Ravenhill, pp. 60-84. New York: Columbia Univ. Press.

Hakim, Peter. 1986. "The Baker Plan: Unfulfilled Promises." *Challenge* 29 (September-October): 55-59.

Harden, Blaine. 1987. "Nigeria: Welcome To Harder Times." *Washington Post National Weekly Edition* (23 March): 18-19.

Hardy, Chandra S. 1986. "Africa's Debt: Structural Adjustment with Stability." In *Strategies for African Development*, ed. Robert J. Berg and Jennifer Seymour Whitaker, pp. 453-75. Berkeley: Univ. of California Press.

Helleiner, G.K. 1983. *The IMF and Africa in the 1980s*. Essays in International Finance no. 152. Princeton: Princeton Univ. Press.

———, ed. 1986. *Africa and the International Monetary Fund.* Washington, D.C.: International Monetary Fund.

Hino, Hiroyuki. 1986. "IMF-World Bank Collaboration." *Finance and Development* 23 (September): 10-14.

Hodges, Tony, Gerald Bourke, and Patricia de Mowbray. 1988. "AFDB Proposes Bold Debt Refinancing Scheme." *Africa Recovery* 2, no. 1 (March): 26-27.

Honeywell, Martin, ed. 1983. *The Poverty Brokers: The IMF and Latin America.* London: Latin American Bureau.

Hoole, Francis. 1977. "Evaluating the Impacts of International Organizations." *International Organization* 33: 541-63.

Huang, Po-Wen, Jr. 1975. *The Asian Development Bank: Diplomacy and Development in Asia.* New York: Vantage Press.

Hunt, Christopher. 1988. "Japan's Financial Clout Is Threatening U.S. Sway at Asian Development Bank." *Wall Street Journal* (23 May): 10.

Hürni, Bettin S. 1980. *The Lending Policy of the World Bank in the 1970's: Analysis and Evaluation.* Boulder: Westview.

Hye, Cheah Cheng. 1988. "U.S. Ambassador Criticizes Policies of Lending Agency." *Wall Street Journal* (15 March): 28.

"IADB Approves Borrowing by Chile as U.S. Abstains." 1986. *Wall Street Journal* (3 December): 31.

Inter-American Development Bank. Various years. *Annual Report.*

International Monetary Fund. Various years. *Annual Report.*

———. Various years. *Balance of Payments Yearbook.*

Jackson, Robert H., and Carl G. Rosberg. 1982. *Personal Rule in Black Africa: Autocrat, Prophet, Tyrant.* Berkeley: Univ. of California Press.

Jacobson, Harold K., William M. Reisinger, and Todd Mathers. 1986. "National Entanglements in International Governmental Organizations." *American Political Science Review* 80, no. 1 (March): 141-59.

Jönsson, Christer. 1986. "Interorganization Theory and International Organization." *International Studies Quarterly* 30: 39-57.

Karns, Margaret P., and Karen A. Mingst. 1987. "International Organizations and Foreign Policy: Influence and Instrumentality." In *New Directions in Foreign Policy,* ed. C.F. Hermann, C.W. Kegley, Jr. and James N. Rosenau, pp. 454-74. Boston: Allen and Unwin.

———. 1990. *The United States and Multilateral Institutions: Patterns of Changing Instrumentality and Influence.* Boston: Unwin Hyman.

Kidder, Peabody and Co., Corporate Finance. 1984. *African Development Bank.* May.

Killick, Tony. 1984. *The IMF and Stabilization: Developing Country Experiences.* New York: St. Martin's Press.

Krasner, Stephen D. 1981. "Power Structures and Regional Development Banks." *International Organization* 35, no. 2 (Spring): 303-28.

Kratochwil, Friedrich, and John Gerard Ruggie. 1986. "International Organization: A State of the Art on an Art of the State." *International Organization* 40, no. 4 (Autumn): 753-75.

Lellouche, Pierre, and Dominique Moisi. 1979. "French Policy in Africa: A Lonely Battle against Destablization." *International Security* 3 (Spring): 108-33.

Loong, Pauline. 1987. "Reaganomics Put ADB under Fire." *Euromoney* (April): 267-71.

Mason, Edward S., and Robert E. Asher. 1973. *The World Bank since Bretton Woods.* Washington, D.C.: Brookings Institution.

Matecki, B.E. 1957. *Establishment of the International Finance Corporation and United States Policy: A Case Study in International Organization.* New York: Praeger.

Meltzer, Ronald. 1976. "The Politics of Policy Reversal: The U.S. Response to Granting Trade Preferences to Developing Countries and Linkages between International Organizations and National Policy Making." *International Organization* 30, no. 4 (Autumn): 649-68.

Mikdashi, Zuhayr. 1972. *The Community of Oil Exporting Countries. A Study in Cooperation.* Ithaca: Cornell Univ. Press.

Mingst, Karen A. 1987. "Inter-Organizational Politics: The World Bank and the African Development Bank." *Review of International Studies* 13, pp. 281-93.

Mingst, Karen A., and Daniel Bon. 1980. "French Intervention in Africa: Dependency or Decolonization." *Africa Today* 27 (2): 5-20.

Mingst, Karen A., and Michael G. Schechter. 1985. "Assessing Intergovernmental Organization Impact: Problems and Prospects." *Review of International Studies* 11: 199-206.

Mitrany, David. 1943. *A Working Peace System.* London: Royal Institute of International Affairs.

Mosley, Paul. 1986. "The Politics of Economic Liberalization: USAID and the World Bank in Kenya, 1980-84." *African Affairs* 85, no. 338 (January): 107-19.

Mvioki, Babutana M. 1985. "Le Statut juridique des opérations du Fonds Africain de Développement." Ph.D. dissertation, Brussels.

N'Diaye, Babacar. 1985. *Swearing In and Investiture of Mr. Babacar N'Diaye as Fifth President of the African Development Bank Group.* Abidjan. 31 August.

Ness, Gayl D., and Steven R. Brechin. 1988. "Bridging the Gap: International Organizations as Organizations." *International Organization* 42, no. 2 (Spring): 245-73.

Nierop, Tom. 1989. "Macro-regions and the Global Institutional Network, 1950-1980." *Political Geography Quarterly* 8, no. 1 (January): 43-65.

"OAU: No Distractions Please." 1985. *West Africa* (29 July): 1529-31.

Oliver, Robert W. 1975. *International Economic Co-operation and the World Bank.* London: Macmillan.

Organization of African Unity. 1980. *The Lagos Plan of Action for the Implementation of the Monrovia Strategy for the Economic Development of Africa.* Adopted by the Second Extraordinary Assembly of OAU Heads of State and Government Devoted to Economic Matters, Lagos, 28-29 April.

Parker, Robert. 1986. "African Development Bank." *Institutional Investor* (April): 1-16.

Payer, Cheryl. 1974. *The Debt Trap: The IMF and the Third World.* New York: Monthly Review Press.

———. 1982. *The World Bank: A Critical Analysis.* New York: Monthly Review Press.

Pine, Art. 1987a. "U.S. Abandons Expansion Plan for the IADB." *Wall Street Journal* (10 April): 18.

———. 1987b. "U.S. Faces Showdown over Bid to Gain Power to Override Loans at the IADB." *Wall Street Journal* (20 March): 8.

Please, Stanley. 1984. *The Hobbled Giant: Essays on the World Bank.* Boulder: Westview.

Please, Stanley, and K.Y. Amoako. 1986. "OAU, ECA and the World Bank: Do They Really Disagree?" In *Africa in Economic Crisis*, ed. John Ravenhill, pp. 127-48. New York: Columbia Univ. Press.

Pratt, Paul. 1982. *Lending and Procurement Policies of the Major International Financing Institutions.* Washington, D.C.: Machinery and Allied Products Institute.

Price Waterhouse Associates. 1977. *African Development Fund Review of Disbursement Procedures.* 14 September.

Rafferty, Kevin. 1985. "Giving a Boost to Privatization." *Institutional Investor* 19 (April): 187-88.

Ravenhill, John. 1986a. "Africa's Continuing Crises: The Elusiveness of Development." In *Africa in Economic Crisis*, ed. John Ravenhill, pp. 1-43. New York: Columbia Univ. Press.

———. 1986b. "Collective Self-Reliance or Collective Self-Delusion: Is the Lagos Plan a Viable Alternative? " In *Africa in Economic Crisis*, ed. John Ravenhill, pp. 85-107. New York: Columbia Univ. Press.

Rogers, Joe. 1986. "Pay Not for Asian Protectionism." *Wall Street Journal* (22 September): 22.

Rosenau, James. 1966. "Pre-Theories and Theories of Foreign Policy." In *Approaches to Comparative and International Politics*, ed. R. Barry Farrell, pp. 27-92. Evanston, Il.: Northwestern Univ. Press.

———. 1986. "Before Cooperation: Hegemons, Regimes and Habit-Driven Actors in World Politics." *International Organization* 40 (Autumn): 849-94.

Rosett, Claudia. 1988. "Soviets Bank on Asian Development." *Wall Street Journal* (9 May): 17.

Rothstein, Robert L. 1979. *Global Bargaining: UNCTAD and the Quest for a New International Economic Order*. Princeton: Princeton Univ. Press.

Rowley, Anthony. 1985. "Ideology before Need." *Far Eastern Economic Review* 127 (14 February): 72-73.

Rule, Sheila. 1987. "Zambian Dispute with I.M.F. Mirrors African Debt Worries." *New York Times* (8 June): 1, 4.

Sanford, Jonathan E. 1982. *U.S. Foreign Policy and Multilateral Development Banks*. Boulder: Westview.

Schoultz, Lars. 1981. *Human Rights and United States Policy toward Latin America*. Princeton, N.J.: Princeton Univ. Press.

———. 1982. "Politics, Economics, and U.S. Participation in Multilateral Development Banks." *International Organization* 36, no. 3 (Summer): 537-74.

Sciolino, Elaine. 1986. "U.N. in Agreement on Steps to Bring African Recovery." *New York Times* (2 June): 1, 8.

Selim, Hussan M. 1983. *Development Assistance Policies and the Performance of Aid Agencies: Studies in the Performance of DAC, OPEC, the Regional Development Banks and the World Bank Group*. New York: St. Martin's Press.

Sesay, Amadu, Olusola Ojo, and Orobola Fasehun. 1984. *The OAU after Twenty Years*. Boulder: Westview.

Snidal, Duncan. 1990. "IGOs, Regimes and Cooperation: Challenges for International Relations Theory." In *The United States and Multilateral Institutions: Patterns of Changing Instrumentality and Influence*, ed. Margaret P. Karns and Karen A. Mingst, pp. 321-50. Boston: Unwin Hyman.

Spiro, Elizabeth P. 1979. "Front Door or Back Stairs: U.S. Human Rights

Policy in the International Financial Institutions." In *Human Rights and U.S. Foreign Policy*, ed. Barry M. Rubin and Elizabeth P. Spiro, pp. 133-61. Boulder: Westview.

Staniland, Martin. 1987. "Francophone Africa: The Enduring French Connection." *Annals of the American Academy of Political and Social Science* 489 (January): 51-62.

Swedberg, Richard. 1986. "The Doctrine of Economic Neutrality of the IMF and the World Bank." *Journal of Peace Research* 23, no. 4 (December): 377-90.

Thurow, Roger. 1989. "Development Bank in Africa Transcends the Region's Despair." *Wall Street Journal* (16 May): 1, 11.

United Nations Economic Commission on Africa. 1987. *The Abuja Statement*. International Conference on Africa: The Challenge of Economic Recovery and Accelerated Development, Abuja, Nigeria, 15-19 June. Addis Ababa.

"United Nations Programme of Action for African Economic Recovery 1986-1990." 1986. *UN Chronicle* 23, no. 4 (August): 7-18.

United States Agency for International Development. 1985. *Project Grant Agreement between the African Development Bank and the United States of America*. AID Project no. 698-0434.

United States Congressional Research Service. 1974. *The United States and the Multilateral Development Banks*. Prepared for the Committee on Foreign Affairs, 93rd Cong., 2d sess. March. Washington, D.C.: U.S. Government Printing Office.

United States Department of the Treasury. 1982. "United States Participation in the Multilateral Banks in the 1980's." Washington, D.C.: U.S. Government Printing Office. February.

United States House of Representatives. 1983. 98th Cong., 1st Sess. *Multilateral Development Bank Act of 1983*. Report No. 98-178.

———. 1985. 99th Cong., 1st Sess. *Multilateral Development Bank Act of 1985*. Report No. 99-122.

———. 1986. 99th Cong., 2nd Sess. Hearings Subcommittee on International Development Institutions and Finance, Committee on Banking, Finance and Urban Affairs. *Multilateral Development Bank Lending for Africa*. Serial No. 99-95.

United States Senate. 1981. 97th Cong., 1st sess. *U.S. Participation in the International Bank for Reconstruction and Development, and Inter-American Development Bank and the Asian Development Fund*. Report No. 97-76. 15 May.

United States Senate Committee on Foreign Relations. 1968. *Inter-*

American Development Bank Capital Stock. Hearings, 90th Cong.,
2nd sess.
_____. 1977. Staff Report to the Subcommittee on Foreign Assistance.
*U.S. Policy and the Multilateral Banks: Politicization and Effec-
tiveness.* Washington, D.C.: U.S. Government Printing Office (95th
Cong., 1st sess.).
Whitaker, Jennifer Seymour. 1986. "The Policy Setting: Crisis and Con-
sensus." In *Strategies for African Development*, ed. Robert J. Berg and
Jennifer Seymour Whitaker, pp. 1-22. Berkeley: Univ. of California
Press.
_____. 1988. *How Can Africa Survive?* New York: Council on Foreign
Relations Press.
White, John. 1972. *Regional Development Banks: The Asian, African
and Inter-American Development Banks.* New York: Praeger.
Williams, Douglas. 1987. *The Specialized Agencies and the United
Nations: The System in Crisis.* New York: St. Martin's Press.
Williamson, John. 1982. *The Lending Policies of the International
Monetary Fund.* Washington, D.C.: Institute for International Eco-
nomics.
Wilson, Dick. 1987. *A Bank for Half the World: The Story of the Asian
Development Bank, 1966-1986.* Manila: Asian Development Bank.
Wodie, Francis. 1984. "The African Development Bank and the African
Development Fund." In *Regional African Organizations*, ed.
Domenico Mazzeo, pp. 85-102. Cambridge: Cambridge Univ. Press.
World Bank. 1945. *Articles of Agreement of the International Bank for
Reconstruction and Development.* Washington, D.C.: IBRD.
_____. 1981a. *Accelerated Development in Sub-Saharan Africa: An
Agenda for Action.* Report No. 3358. August.
_____. 1981b. *World Development Report.*
_____. 1983. *World Tables.* Washington, D.C.
_____. 1984. *Toward Sustained Development in Sub-Saharan Africa:
A Joint Program of Action.* Washington, D.C.
_____. 1985. "Outcome of Discussions with AFDB Delegation." Con-
sultation Meeting of 14-16 January on Aid Coordination. Un-
published document.
_____. 1986. *Financing Adjustment with Growth in Sub-Saharan Af-
rica, 1986-1990.* Washington, D.C.
_____. Various years. *Annual Report.* Washington, D.C.
Yasutomo, Dennis T. 1983. *Japan and the Asian Development Bank.*
New York: Praeger.

Zulu, Jostin B., and Saleh M. Nsouli. 1985. *Adjustment Programs in Africa: The Recent Experience.* IMF Occasional Paper No. 34. Washington, D.C. April.

Interviews

G. Aithnard, Training, African Development Bank (hereafter ADB).
Mme. Bak-hansen, UNDP.
A.I. Barry, Chief, Evaluation Division, ADB.
M. Bouzid, Country Programmes, ADB.
S. Bunyasi, Economic Development Institute, World Bank.
A. Carr, Consultant, Anthony Carr and Assoc.
J. Conrow, U.S. Department of the Treasury.
Mme. S. Diarra, Information Division, ADB.
D. Etounga, Louis Berger International.
R. Free, U.S. Department of the Treasury.
F. Gentile, Campagnia Generale Progettazions E. Installazioni, Milan.
Mr. Gnoukoury, Conseil de l'Entente.
T. Kaaria, Executive Director (Finland), ADB.
Mr. Kahangi, Control Project Services, ADB.
Mr. Kasonga, Economics & Country Programs, ADB.
S. Kpognon, West African Division, World Bank.
M. Malamo, Division of Information, ADB.
E. McCoy, Alternate Executive Director (USA), ADB.
Mr. Melanie, Director, Personnel Training, ADB.
H.N.M. Narobi, Dept. of Cooperation and Information, ADB.
E. Ndahimana, Executive Director (Rwanda), ADB.
G. Nguionzu, Executive Director (Cameroon), ADB.
Mr. Nnebe-Agumadu, Country Programmes, ADB.
N.E. Nolan, REDSO, USAID.
K. Nyahe, Division of Agriculture and Rural Development, ADB.
S. Omari, Planning & Research Department, ADB.
T. Ouattara, Department of Finance, ADB.
Mr. Peterson, Alternate Executive Director (Sweden), ADB.
G. Proulx, Executive Director (Canada), ADB.
D. Rwedgasira, Planning & Research Department, ADB.
J. Schneider, REDSO/USAID.
D. Sherk, Executive Director (U.S.), ADB.
O. Shimizu, Executive Director (Japan), ADB.
Mr. N.N. Susungi, Division of Industry & Development Bank, ADB.
Mr. B.W. West, Vice Consul, Embassy of Great Britain.
Mr. Zeleke, Country Programs, ADB.

Index

African Development Bank (ADB): African character of, 57, 58; Agreement Establishing the African Development Bank, 3, 8, 16, 30, 32; agricultural policy, 62, 63-66; Arab/Islamic organizations, relations with, 135; bilateral aid agencies, relations with, 136-39; board of governors, 30-32; conditionality, 74-75, 80, 127, 130, 139; constraints on influence: environmental, 82-84, organizational, 85-87, 88, 143-44, 148, political, 15, 49, 89-100; debt issues, 129, 134; economic resources of, 9-10; evaluation, 143-49; executive directors (board of directors), 32-39, 48, 60, 74; extraregional members, 10, 13, 54, 55-58, 59-62, 97-99; financial rating of, 59, 77; financial preconditions, 72-73, 86; General Conditions Applicable to Loan and Guarantee Agreements, 47; lack of influence, 69, 70; language issue, 31, 85; legitimacy of, 76, 113-14, 115, 186; "linking-pin status", 102, 112, 114; literature on, 7-8; loan disbursement, 48-49, 86-87; loan distribution patterns, 66, 89-92, 170-71; loan negotiations, 47-48, 71, 73, 79-80, 95; Manual of Operating Procedures, 43; non-project lending, 50, 75, 80, 85, 86, 107, 149; political resources, 13, 15, 17; president, 19-24 (see also Fordwor, K.D.; N'Diaye, B.); privatization, 70-71; procurement, 95-97; project procedures, 43-44, 45-47, 86; regional offices, 21, 83; regional (multinational) projects, 51-53, 84; sanctions for arrears, 77-79, 80, 86; secretariat, 24-30, 92-94; and United States, 17, 157-58; voting in, 15-16

African Development Fund (ADF), 7, 13, 40, 46, 55, 58, 65, 77, 78, 146, 150, 153, 161; history of, 11-12; legal relationship with African Development Bank, 39-40; voting in, 16-17

African development organizations, 133-35, 140

Africanicity, 14, 18, 79

Africa's Priority Program for Economic Recovery (APPER), 133

agriculture in Africa, 61